DEDICATED TO LOVE, LEARNING AND LEADERSHIP

BARRY
UNIVERSITY

1940-2000

BY PRUDY TAYLOR BOARD

THE
DONNING COMPANY
PUBLISHERS

DEDICATED TO LOVE, LEARNING AND LEADERSHIP

BARRY
U N I V E R S I T Y

1940-2000

BY PRUDY TAYLOR BOARD

The Donning Company Publishers
184 Business Park Drive, Suite 206
Virginia Beach, VA 23462

Steve Mull, General Manager
B. L. Walton Jr., Project Director
Robin E. Neff, Project Research Coordinator
Dawn V. Kofroth, Assistant General Manager
Sally Clarke Davis, Editor
Marshall Rouse McClure, Graphic Designer
John Harrell, Imaging Artist
Scott Rule, Senior Marketing Coordinator
Patricia Peterson, Marketing Coordinator

Library of Congress Cataloging-in-Publication Data

1-57864-119-5

Printed in the United States of America

4

TABLE OF CONTENTS

FOREWORD

For 60 years Barry University has provided an educational, cultural, and religious refuge and oasis from the tensions and stresses of inner city Miami-Dade.

My own first immersion in Barry came in the 1960s. I attended (at that time) Barry College studying courses required for certification to teach secondary school English. At that time the instructors were mainly nuns who wore their habits in class. The only on-campus students were female. There was such an environment of spiritual tranquility during those days. Today, even with the school 10 times the size as the 1960s, that same calm atmosphere prevails.

Since those days Barry has extended its philosophy and spirit into our South Florida community. It has become a stabilizing force during the turbulent times we have experienced. Sister Jeanne and her staff have become positive symbols of leadership so badly needed.

Barry University has benefited South Florida and the Caribbean—in fact the whole United States and the world. But primarily I cannot envision Miami-Dade without Barry. For without Barry University South Florida would be a much lesser place.

There are various facilities in Miami-Dade and elsewhere that bear my name—but having a building at Barry University with my name is the greatest honor for public service anyone can possibly receive.

Thank you Barry University.

William Lehman
United States House of Representatives, 1972–1992

ACKNOWLEDGMENTS

Working on a project such as the history of a university that has meant so much to its community, is a tremendous challenge. I was left with a sense of awe and appreciation for the enormous number of lives touched and made better by their association with Barry University. It was a privilege to have been given the opportunity to help create this history and I am grateful.

My heartfelt thanks for their patience, kindness, efficiency, and never-failing assistance go to the archivists Sister Dorothy Jehle, OP; Sister Jean Kathleen Comiskey, OP; Irene Maliga. Michele Morris, Assistant Vice President for University Relations, was always helpful and willing to research even the most minute detail. The research and interviews done by Sister Eileen F. Rice, OP, were absolutely invaluable and formed the backbone of this book. Special thanks are also due my friend Sharon McGrath who helped me organize the mountains of material and Sally Davis, my editor at Donning. My hope is that the readers will enjoy this book as much as I enjoyed writing it.

Prudy Taylor Board
Delray Beach, Florida
July 1, 2000

INTRODUCTION

Imagine what Mother Gerald Barry and her brothers Monsignor William Barry and Bishop Patrick Barry would say if they could see us now! Despite the Great Depression they—and their friend John Thompson—dreamed of building a Catholic college for women in Florida. That dream has evolved into today's 8,000-student, coeducational university with a medical school, a law school, and even national championship athletic teams. Many thousands of people have created the history of Barry University, yet we remain true to our early roots as a Catholic, international institution.

From the very start, Adrian Dominican Sisters were the executives, construction bosses, and teachers. They helped turn Florida scrub pine-covered land into the core campus that started with 45 full-time students in 1940. Barry's 60-year history is lush with examples of Adrian Dominican sacrifice; my Sisters' contributions—intellectual, financial, and spiritual—have built Barry's success. Today the Congregation continues to sponsor us.

Barry has never before published a history book. *Barry University, 1940–2000: Dedicated to Love, Learning and Leadership* celebrates our first 60 years with entertaining, enlightening photos and text. Sr. Eileen F. Rice, OP, spent more than 10 years gathering interviews. Her untiring work gave author Prudy Taylor Board insight and "color" from firsthand sources.

This year's Diamond Jubilee theme is "60 Years in Florida, One Student at a Time." I think that summarizes Barry's greatest accomplishment—educating students in a caring, personal way. I believe that Barry University has helped shape our society's past, and the best of our past only hints at the promise of our future.

I hope you'll enjoy reading this book. If you spent time here at Barry, especially as a student, you might see pictures that remind you of those days—classmates, favorite professors, buildings or rooms, traditional activities. If so, my prayer is that they bring back pleasant memories and help you relive the history that you helped create.

Happy reading and God bless you all,

Sr. Jeanne O'Laughlin, OP, Ph.D.
President, Barry University

Barry College's eighteenth birthday was celebrated with reverence on November 20, 1958. The Most Rev. Coleman F. Carroll (seated far left in the photo) offered a Pontifical High Mass in Cor Jesu Chapel. The Founders Day program was held and Mother Gerald, OP, (standing right) that morning conferred an honorary Doctor of Laws degree upon Bishop Carroll who was the first Bishop of Miami. At the same ceremony, the Barry College Laudare Medal was awarded to James A. Brennan, Sr. (standing left). Brennan was head of the Brennan Construction Company which constructed several of Barry's buildings including the Fine Arts wing and the auditorium. Rev. John F. Monroe, OP, (center), professor of theology and philosophy, served as chairman of the program. Also on stage was Sister Mary Alice Collins, OP, executive vice president. She served as dean from 1953 to August 1958, when she became executive vice president and was closely involved with students and active in areas such as recruitment, admissions, and scheduling as well as advising students.

CHAPTER ONE
Valiant Dreams, Valiant Women

The Barry College graduate is expected to be "a valiant woman and to put out
her hand to strong things." Earnestness of purpose and consistency in effort
are expected of all. This does not mean that there is an atmosphere of
gloom and repression but rather that the spirit of abundant gladness that comes
from the accomplishment of worthwhile things dominates the campus.
— Barry College 1940-41 Catalog

Mother Gerald Barry, Prioress General of the Dominican Sisters of Adrian, Michigan, was—along with her brothers Patrick and William—cofounder and first president of Barry College. She was born in Ireland in 1881, came to America in 1900 and attended Northwestern University and Detroit Teachers' College, receiving a bachelor's degree from Siena Heights in Adrian. Mother Gerald entered the Dominican Order in 1912 and was elected mother general in 1933. Serving in this position for twenty-eight years, she became ex officio president of Barry College when it opened in 1940. Since she resided in Adrian, she appointed successive executive vice presidents to administer the affairs of the college. In 1950, Pope Pius XII awarded Mother Gerald the Lateran Cross for outstanding service to the Church. She died on November 20, 1961.

Officially, Barry College opened its doors in September 1940 with an open house on Friday the 13th. A hurricane lurked in the Atlantic, but neither the weather nor the date challenged the faith or dampened the enthusiasm of the 1,000-plus people who visited the campus that weekend. By Sunday, the hurricane's threat had waned as it veered northward. Monday was an exciting and momentous day as the first students arrived and registered—dashing through intermittent cloudbursts, the hurricane's legacy. Classes started on Thursday, September 19.

According to the Registrar's records, enrollment in the fall of 1940-41 was comprised of twenty-one freshmen, sixteen sophomores and eight juniors. In addition to Florida, students came from Connecticut, Indiana, Michigan, New York, Ohio, Pennsylvania, and Wisconsin. As a liberal arts college, Barry offered eleven majors: English, Latin, French, Spanish, biology, chemistry, mathematics, history, music, home economics, and secretarial science. Minors included philosophy, speech, German, Italian, and education. To obtain a degree, 128 semester hours of credit were required.

The opening of Barry College was the culmination of a long-held, cherished dream of three of its founders—Mother Gerald Barry, OP, and her brothers Monsignor William Barry and Bishop Patrick Barry. As Superior General of the Adrian Dominican Sisters in Adrian, Michigan, Mother Gerald had been making annual visits to Dominican convents in Florida since 1933. She was painfully aware that, while the state was dotted with parochial schools, Florida had no institution of higher education for Catholic girls.

Gifted with zeal, faith, determination, and perseverance, she vowed to establish a college to fill that need. Mother Gerald shared her vision with Bishop Barry, who responded in a letter dated April 27, 1937 which read, in part:

The idea of a woman's college is fine and surely it would be a wonderful thing
if it could be financed. Miami would be a good location but you have to
consider the Miami University (University of Miami). Again, Jacksonville
might be thought of. Building costs, finance for operation, some endorsement,

The Most Reverend Patrick Barry was born in West Clare, Ireland in 1868. He was ordained in 1895 and shortly afterward left to come to Florida as a missionary. First assigned as assistant at the Church of the Immaculate Conception in Jacksonville, he served as a volunteer chaplain during the Spanish-American War. In 1903, Father Barry was appointed pastor at the mission in Palatka, Florida; ten years later, he was named pastor of the new parish of the Assumption in Jacksonville. He served in Jacksonville until 1917 when he was called to St. Augustine and made Vicar-General of the Cathedral. On February 22, 1922, he was proclaimed Bishop of St. Augustine by Pope Pius XI. He was responsible for the establishment of sixteen churches, several hospitals, an orphans' home, and a mission church for Black Catholics in Florida.

teachers qualified, etc., and wise planning and counsel and the survey neces-sary (are all needed) to come to a final conclusion. Never buy a pig in a poke.

Jacksonville was never seriously considered and soon they approached Monsignor Barry, enlisting his aid to find a suitable location in Miami. He turned to John Graves Thompson, a young lawyer with whom he often played handball. In addition to being a friend, Thompson was a partner in the law firm of Thompson & Thompson (later Smathers & Thompson) and also mayor of Miami Shores Village, in 1943-44. Thompson and Monsignor Barry devoted nearly two years searching and ruled out three other sites—including Vizcaya, the James Deering estate—before settling on the present location.

In the spring of 1939, Thompson was charged by Mother Gerald with the task of finding a name for the new school. He suggested Geraldi College, but she rejected that idea and presented a list of alternatives for his and Monsignor Barry's

John Graves Thompson, mayor of Miami Shores in 1944 and cofounder of Barry College, was a law partner of Senator George Smathers. He also served as Barry's legal advisor for many years. In 1956, he was awarded the Barry Laudare Medal as a "praiseworthy citizen of the community" and, in 1958, Barry conferred upon him an honorary Doctor of Laws degree. Born in Bement, Illinois in 1906, he died on April 12, 1962.

consideration. Ultimately, the Board of Trustees in Adrian approved the name of Barry College to honor His Excellency, the Most Reverend Patrick Barry, Bishop of St. Augustine, Florida and college cofounder.

By the time the forty-acre site between 111th and 115th Streets and NE Second and Miami Avenues had been chosen, Thompson was personally committed to the project. In his role as cofounder, he completed the purchase on May 2, 1940, paying $40,000.

Architect Gerald Barry, a nephew, drew plans for the college. These were ratified with minor changes by the General Council of the Adrian Dominicans. The General Council became Barry's Board of Trustees on January 2, 1940, with the authority and responsibility of financing and operating the fledgling college.

Progress now was swift. The groundbreaking was held January 24, 1940, and the day was so cold that Mother Barry decided to install steam heat in the dining hall and the chapel! On February 5, Judge Paul D. Barnes approved the charter.

On June 20, 1940, Bishop Barry blessed the first five buildings. The cornerstones contained copper boxes holding copies of *The Miami Herald*, *The Miami Daily News*, *The Florida Catholic* and other Catholic newspapers along with lists of city, county, and state officials. Imprinted on each cornerstone was the Barry escutcheon created by Sister Helene O'Connor, a certified heraldist from Siena Heights College in Adrian. The design combined the coats of arms of the Barry family and the Dominican Order.

Also present for the blessing of the buildings were Mother Theresa Joseph, Superior-General of the Sisters of St. Joseph of St. Augustine; Mother Magdalena from St. Francis Hospital on Miami Beach; Miami Shores City Manager Lawton McCall; and Frank Wheeler, the contractor.

When the college opened in September, not all the construction was completed. Sister Regina Marie LeLonde, a member of the first faculty, recalled arriving to find " . . . the grounds a rough, sandy mess. The window screens had not been put in and the mosquitoes were biting. So we lived at St. Francis Hospital on Miami Beach until the dormitories were ready." She also recalled that the chapel was not finished so they had Mass in the dining hall until November 1.

Born in West Clare, Ireland in 1886, The Right Reverend Monsignor William Barry studied for the priesthood in Baltimore, Maryland and was ordained there for the Diocese of St. Augustine in 1910. After serving in St. Augustine, Jacksonville, and Deland, Father Barry came to Miami Beach in 1926 to organize a new parish which became St. Patrick's church. Before the church's completion in 1928, Monsignor Barry celebrated masses and school was taught in reconditioned polo stables donated by his lifelong friend, developer Carl G. Fisher. In May 1937, he became a Monsignor and in 1953 was awarded the title of Prothonotary Apostolic. In 1966, he resigned as pastor of St. Patrick's parish after serving more than forty years. Monsignor Barry died shortly after midnight on November 17, 1967. His passing was marked in the secular world by the publication of his eulogy in the *Congressional Record* on December 15 and a letter to the editor written by former Florida Governor Fuller Warren.

Another member of the faculty that first year was Sister Agnes Cecile Prendergast who remembered that only Rosa Mystica was ready for occupancy. She remembered washing their long white habits in the upstairs launderette, carrying them downstairs, and then hanging them on ropes strung between trees. The ropes would sometimes break, the habits would fall into the sand, and they would have to be carried upstairs and washed again.

As landscaping and construction continued that October, Sister Gonzaga

This photo of Northeast Second Avenue reveals how rural and undeveloped the area was in the late 1930s. The property on the left side of the avenue later became the site of Barry College.

This snapshot was taken in 1940 shortly before construction of the entrance on Northeast Second Avenue was completed.

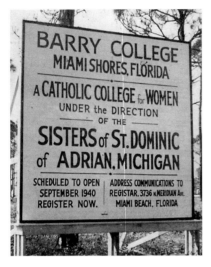

It was a happy day for everyone concerned when this sign was erected on the site.

Mother Gerald (center) was an active participant at the groundbreaking on January 24, 1940.

The heavy coats and hats the men wore during the groundbreaking were mute evidence that the day was frosty and that the normally balmy breezes were biting and brisk.

Greene, business manager and construction supervisor, confronted a workman delivering a load of black dirt. In the meantime, Sister Rita Cecile Boyle, wearing her long white habit, climbed into the truck bed. She had been called from her mathematics class to measure the dirt. She assured Sister Gonzaga that even though the bill the workman presented was for five yards of dirt, the truck contained only three and a half. Sister Gonzaga immediately deducted 1.5 yards from the invoices for each truckload of dirt that had been delivered. The workman did not argue with her.

Inconvenience was a way of life that first year and yet Barry moved forward. In October, the college offered evening and Saturday classes in modern languages, secretarial science, and art. In November, the *Barry College Digest*—the student newspaper known today as *The Buccaneer*—was launched. On November 3, the Barry faculty entertained the faculty from the University of Miami at tea and on November 17, Sister Denise Mainville broadcast the first of a series of piano concerts over radio station WIOD. Barry College was well and happily launched and, from the earliest days, stretched welcoming hands to its community and its neighbors.

Christmas that first year was certainly not a vacation for the Sisters. Once the students returned to their homes for the holidays, the Sisters began cleaning the residence halls. Although men did the heavy cleaning, the Sisters did the rest because they couldn't afford additional help. The Sisters also sang Christmas carols

On site, Gerald Barry, A. I. A. (left), studied the plans he'd drawn for Barry College's first five buildings while the priests looked on. Barry was based in Chicago, Illinois with the firm of Barry and Kay. Barry died June 9, 1966 while vacationing in Montreal, Canada.

The grounds were indeed barren in this photo taken during construction that summer of 1940. Cor Jesu Chapel is in the center.

This close-up view of Cor Jesu Chapel, taken July 20, 1940, reveals the care, dedication, and precision with which the buildings were constructed.

When dedicated on February 4, 1941, these five buildings comprised the Barry campus: a) Cor Jesu Chapel; b) Angelicus, the classroom-administration unit, named in honor of St. Thomas, the Angelic Doctor; c) Calaroga, the dining hall, named for the birthplace of St. Dominic; d) Maris Stella (Star of the Sea) and e) Rosa Mystica (Mystical Rose), dormitories. The dormitories all bore the titles of the Virgin Mary.

Skies were sunny and serene and construction was on schedule.

at the Firestone Estate at the request of Monsignor Barry and held the first Christmas party in Florida for the Dominican Sisters.

As students returned to campus after the Christmas vacation, everyone pitched in to help prepare for the dedication of the college scheduled for February 4, 1941. After weeks of preparation the day dawned and it was a happy event. The ceremony began with the Apostolic Delegate, Archbishop Amleto Cicognani, leading the procession and celebrating the Mass. This was followed by a sermon by Archbishop John T. McNicholas, then a banquet after which Bishop Joseph P. Hurley of St. Augustine spoke.

After Bishop Hurley's comments, the students presented a program featuring Sister Denise's musical composition titled "Welcome," student Eleanor Neary's "Greetings" and "End and Beginning," a play by John Masefield.

As Sister Eileen Rice, OP, wrote in *Barry University: Its Beginnings*, "For the founders, Dedication Day fulfilled a dream which they had discussed in the Adrian Dominican Generalate in Michigan, debated in the Barry home in County Clare, Ireland, continued in John Thompson's law offices in Miami, and planned in St. Patrick's Rectory in Miami Beach."

Further, Sister Eileen reports that an editorial in *The Florida Catholic* discussed Barry's "unlimited possibilities," not only for Florida but for the whole of the U.S.A. and " . . . beyond our borders to the South." The editorial read, in part:

Latin America is much in the mind and plans of the people of the North just now, and what more natural than to visualize great numbers of South

Blessings and prayers graced each step of the fledgling college's growth. This photo, taken following the laying of the five cornerstones on June 20, 1940, marked—in retrospect—an especially poignant occasion because it was Bishop Patrick Barry's final public appearance. He blessed and applied the first layer of mortar on the cornerstone for each of the buildings. Two months later on August 13, 1940 he died at the age of seventy-two.

American young women pursuing learning and culture in our new college, seeking the ancient and soul-sustaining wisdom of the surroundings.

Those statements proved to be prescient, for on May 2, the students initiated Barry College's program of Pan American relations when the sociology department presented a symposium on peace.

Five student societies were begun that year—the Sodality; Tara Singers; Press Association; Verse Speaking Choir; and the Hobby Club. Traditional events inaugurated included formal investiture in cap and gown; Christmas caroling; the tree planting ceremony; St. Thomas Aquinas Symposium; St. Patrick's Day as Freshman Class Day; Retreat; crowning of the campus queen; College Day for incoming students; coronation of the Blessed Virgin statue in Cor Jesu Chapel; sophomore spring formal which became the Spring prom; and the baccalaureate and rose and candle ceremonies.

There was no graduation ceremony to mark the successful conclusion to Barry College's first year because there were no seniors. However, an honors convocation was held in the rotunda. After Mass and breakfast, the students headed home. The date was June 5, 1941.

Even that first summer was eventful. A couple of weeks after the students left,

Invitations were dispatched to the ceremonies commemorating the laying of the cornerstones.

THE SISTERS OF ST. DOMINIC
OF ADRIAN, MICHIGAN
REQUEST THE HONOR OF YOUR PRESENCE AT THE
CEREMONY OF THE LAYING OF THE CORNER STONES
OF

BARRY COLLEGE
THURSDAY MORNING, JUNE TWENTIETH
NINETEEN HUNDRED AND FORTY

AT TEN-THIRTY O'CLOCK

NORTHEAST SECOND AVENUE AT ONE HUNDRED ELEVENTH STREET
MIAMI, FLORIDA

HIS EXCELLENCY
THE MOST REVEREND PATRICK BARRY, D.D.
WILL PRESIDE

Barry inaugurated an annual tradition of holding a summer retreat for the Adrian Dominican women religious in Florida. On June 23, Barry held its first six-week summer program staffed by a faculty augmented by Adrian Dominicans who worked during the regular school year in the northern schools.

Miami was tranquil that warm September when Barry students returned for the second year, but the bombing of Pearl Harbor on December 7 destroyed that tranquility. Barry students gathered around the pool late that warm December

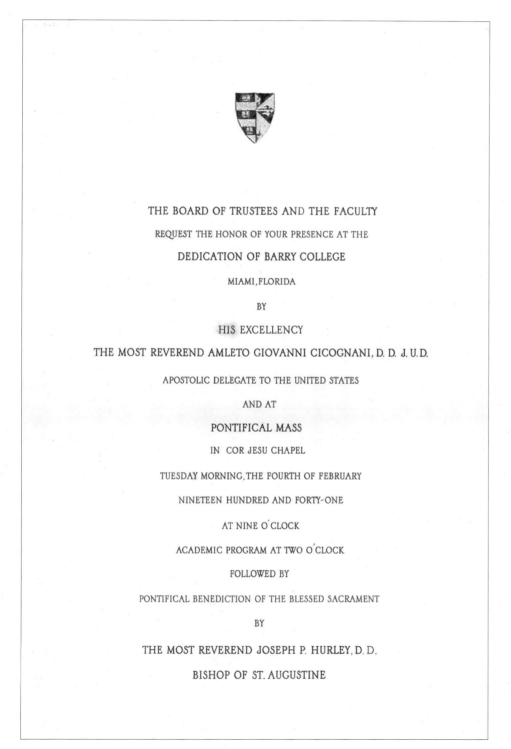

THE BOARD OF TRUSTEES AND THE FACULTY

REQUEST THE HONOR OF YOUR PRESENCE AT THE

DEDICATION OF BARRY COLLEGE

MIAMI, FLORIDA

BY

HIS EXCELLENCY

THE MOST REVEREND AMLETO GIOVANNI CICOGNANI, D. D. J. U. D.

APOSTOLIC DELEGATE TO THE UNITED STATES

AND AT

PONTIFICAL MASS

IN COR JESU CHAPEL

TUESDAY MORNING, THE FOURTH OF FEBRUARY

NINETEEN HUNDRED AND FORTY-ONE

AT NINE O'CLOCK

ACADEMIC PROGRAM AT TWO O'CLOCK

FOLLOWED BY

PONTIFICAL BENEDICTION OF THE BLESSED SACRAMENT

BY

THE MOST REVEREND JOSEPH P. HURLEY, D. D.

BISHOP OF ST. AUGUSTINE

Because of the importance of the occasion, engraved invitations were sent to Barry College's dedication. The roster of participants and attendees reveals that it was an extremely significant event drawing The Most Reverend Amleto Giovanni Cicognani, Apostolic Delegate to the United States.

afternoon when news of the attack was broadcast on the radio. Father Cyril Burke, OP, the new Dominican chaplain, was on hand to talk with the students who were stunned by the devastating news.

World War II brought fear and tragedy along with shortages and rationing. But it had its lighter moments as well, according to a work-in-progress by Sister Eileen F. Rice, OP. For example, Sister Mary Jane Hart, who taught chemistry and biology, was a graduate of Institutum Divi Thomae in Cincinnati and, as such, was involved in scientific research. When local police learned this, officers frequently brought her dead snakes they thought might be helpful in her work. Alas, Sister Mary Jane could not find a way to preserve them so she and Sister Rita Cecile Boyle sometimes dug holes in the ground behind the library where they buried the decomposing reptiles.

Sister Eileen also records that the Institutum wanted shark liver oil which was used in Biodyne ointment, some vitamins, and petrolatum. Sisters Mary Jane and Rita Cecile worked during the dinner hour because the processing of the oil was a dirty, odoriferous task. Sometimes, they worked until after dark. In peacetime, this would not have created a problem. However, after the United States entered World War II on September 8, 1941, the law required that blackout curtains be installed on every window in every building on campus.

The Sisters, working in the lab in Adrian Hall, would sometimes become so

Shortly before the school's opening on September 19, 1940, finishing touches including sod and land-scaping transformed Angelicus Hall (now Adrian Hall).

engrossed in their work that they would forget to close the curtains on the windows which faced NE Second Avenue. When they forgot three nights in a row, the chief of police appeared and, according to Sister Rita Cecile's taped memoirs, threatened to arrest them if they did not shut the curtains.

During the war years dances on the campus were held in the students' dining room in what is now LaVoie Hall. After dinner, students and faculty carried out tables and decorated the room. After the dance, the young women changed into work clothes and helped the Sisters rearrange the furniture and reset the tables for breakfast.

Servicemen who attended the dances included Royal Air Force navigators training at the University of Miami and U.S. Navy pilots from the Opa Locka Naval Station.

Returning alumnae recalled that they were required to wear modest dresses with sleeves and that only nonalcoholic beverages were served. The college administrative staff made a visible presence as chaperones.

Faculty and students—especially those living on campus—were close in the early years. According to a taped interview with Sister Noreen McKeough, when students saw the Sisters preparing for a hurricane, they pitched in to help. Since August and September are typically the most active months of the hurricane season, this was a rather common occurrence.

Academic year 1944-45 became known as the year of the "out houses," so

This brilliantly-colored postcard was very popular during the mid-to-late 1950s. Its caption read, ". . . Situated on an 85-acre tract of land in Miami Shores, a residential suburb, the college offers both graduate and undergraduate programs of studies in the many liberal arts fields."

PRECEDING SPREAD: The 1948–49 Adrian Dominican faculty, staff, and administrators of Barry College. Front (from left): Sisters Dorothy Browne, Mary Ann Rissert, Marie Grace Gibney, executive vice president, Rose Mary McElroy, and Agnes Patrice Waldron. Rear: Sisters Helen Duggan, Elaine Scanlon, Agnes Cecile Prendergast, Mary Jane Hart, Mary Jean Walsh, Marie McGowan, Clarisena Meyer, Denise Mainville, Noreen McKeough, Joanne O'Connor, Thomas Mary Walsh, Eulalia LaVoie, Rose Therese Audretsch, Cleophas Freiburger, Michael James Carter, Jean Marie Sheridan, and Trinita Flood.

dubbed—innocently, of course—by Sister Gonzaga because so many students had to be housed off campus. That year seven houses were rented within a two-mile radius of the college. By the following year, the Gladmor Hotel at 74th Street and Biscayne Boulevard had been commandeered, adding forty beds. In the meantime, ground was broken for Weber Hall (originally known as Stella Matutina), the new dormitory.

World War II ended and peace returned to Miami and Barry College. In the fall of 1946, Sister Marie Grace Gibney succeeded Sister Gonzaga as executive vice president. Growth and change were steady so that by 1950 the population numbered 290 and was comprised of students from twenty states and eight foreign countries including Formosa, China, Japan, Germany, and Iran. In 1952, Sister Edmund Harrison succeeded Sister Marie Grace as executive vice president. In 1953, a Bachelor of Science in Nursing program was inaugurated and four years later, the charter class of nineteen nurses received their degrees. In 1954, a graduate department was opened with courses leading to the Master of Arts degree with a major in English as well as Master of Arts or Science degrees with a major in education. In 1956, as the student population continued growing, the Town and Country Motel located directly opposite Barry College on Second Avenue was purchased.

By 1960, Barry's second decade, the student body had reached 796. The memories of World War II were fading and the campus was placid. Barry's valiant women were striving with sincere earnestness of purpose to achieve the goals set for them twenty years earlier. There was progress—Barry was accepted as a member of the Association of Independent Colleges of Florida that year and, in 1961, was reaccredited by the Southern Association of Colleges. However, change was looming on the horizon and perhaps the harbinger was a sad event—the death of Mother Gerald Barry on November 20, 1961. Mother Genevieve Weber was elected Prioress General and named the second president of Barry College. Within six months, Barry suffered another loss when cofounder John G. Thompson died on April 12, 1962. But the founders had done their work well and the work of the Dominicans and Barry College continued smoothly and without pause. The nursing program was accredited by the National League for Nursing Collegiate Board of Review and the Dalton-Dunspaugh House and Thompson Hall were completed.

However, the change had just begun . . . .

Education majors Barbara Kiep '60 (left) and Janet Burt '60 (right) prepared and mounted posters as part of the process of learning to teach phonics.

BARRY COLLEGE'S INAUGURAL YEAR
1940–1941

Forty-five students enrolled and registered to take the twenty-six courses offered that first year.

The First Faculty

Religion and Philosophy — Reverend J. B. Walker, OP

Religion and English — Sister Francis Joseph Wright, OP

Social Studies — Sister M. Loyola Vath, OP

Romance Languages — Sister Regina Marie LaLonde, OP

Mathematics and Science — Sister M. Rita Cecile Boyle, OP

Latin and History — Sister M. Agnes Cecile Prendergast, OP

Science and Research — Sister Mary Jane Hart, OP

Secretarial Science — Sister Francis Clare O'Brien, OP

Home Economics — Sister Rose Dominic LeBlanc, OP, Miss Helen Meyer

Music — Sister Mary Denise Mainville, OP

Voice — Madame Mary Lenander spent one day each week on campus

Art — Mr. J. Clinton Shepherd

Physical Education — Mrs. Alice Liberto was engaged for two days each week to conduct classes in physical education and various sports

Librarian — Sister Michael James Carter, OP

Superior and Business Manager — Sister Mary Gonzaga Greene, OP

Dean and Registrar — Sister Mary DeLellis Raftrey, OP

President — Mother Gerald Barry, OP

LEFT: Doris Hart, 1951 Wimbledon champion, attended Barry College for two-and-a-half years, matriculating as a freshman in 1943. Known affectionately on campus as "Champ" because she had already won the National Girls Tennis Championship in 1942 and following that both the Junior Woman's Singles and Doubles Championships, she was an inspiration to many because of the courage and determination she displayed despite illness and an injured knee. She is one of the very few players who won the Australian, French, United States, and Wimbledon championships at least once.

ABOVE: Arbor Day in 1952 involved the annual freshman tree planting on the east lawn of Rosa Mystica. The class president threw a shovelful of earth on the sapling's roots and Father Cyril Burke, OP, campus chaplain, sprinkled the tree with holy water and blessed it. The ceremony marked the "fruitful and ever-growing loyalty of the new students to their Alma Mater." Father Burke spent thirty-seven of his fifty-seven years as a priest at Barry. He died May 26, 1997 in Providence, Rhode Island at the age of eighty-eight.

The students attending Barry College were not merely educated, but trained in the social graces as well. Shown here in 1954, the girls hosted a dance in the Fine Arts Building and enjoyed dancing with their escorts on the patio.

The first capping ceremony of Barry College's new nursing department was held January 13, 1955. Sister Helen Margaret McGinley, OP, nursing department chairperson, officiated. Marianne Stadler '57 was among the twenty-one participants. The cap and the candle held special significance. The candle represented the fire of love and unity and, at the same time, the lamp of vigilance associated with Florence Nightingale. The cap was designed to honor the Marian year and featured a creased letter "M" for Mary in the back. The three pleats in the front symbolized the Blessed Trinity and the virtues of faith, hope, and charity. The black monogram comprised of the letters "B" and "C" represented Barry College.

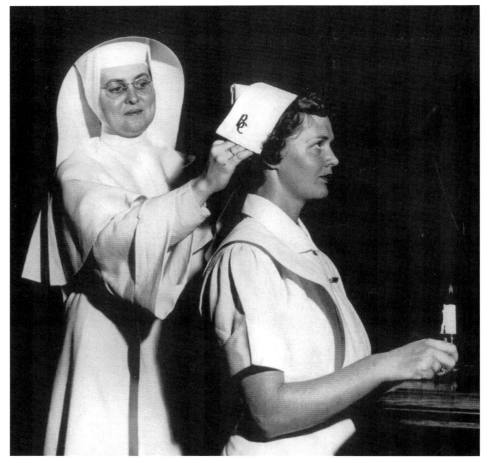

"Check the perspective," Sister Mary Joseph Kennedy, OP, seemed to be saying to one of the members of her 1960 art class.

The Speech and Drama Department has always been one of the most active areas on campus. During the twenty years she chaired this department, Sister Marie Carol Hurley, OP, trained dozens of theatre majors. Shown here with Sister are some of the cast of the original musical "Sweet Mystery" based on the music of Victor Herbert. Barry students seen are Sandra Hovey Schlather '61, Mercedes Molina Mueckenheim '61 (seated), and Rosemary Shirald Carmas '60. The young man was recruited from the Miami area.

An understanding of science was important in order to have a well-rounded education in 1962 and students Marie Burke '63 (left) and Claudia Hauri '64 applied themselves diligently to the Kymograph during the study of muscle physiology for their biology class.

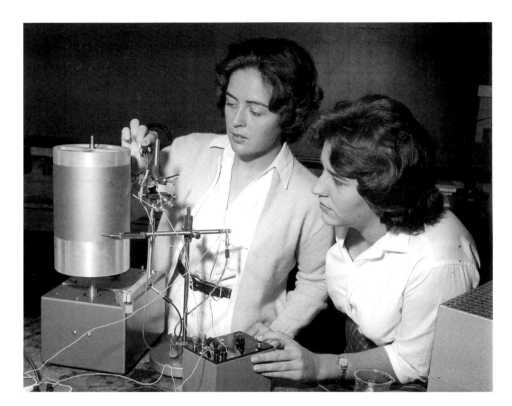

As a science, chemistry was as confusing—if essential—in 1962 as it is today. Judging by the expressions on the faces of these unidentified students, chemistry lab proved to be a difficult and serious subject.

The Barry College Catering Service—membership was restricted to home economics majors—was a popular group and the reason is obvious. Maureen Lathers was taste-testing the cookie icing which Joanne Rerucha was applying while Pat Ace '57 measured ingredients for the punch. In this photo taken in January 1954, they were preparing for a party.

BELOW: In the Foods Class, every step of the preparation process was important, but so was an understanding and knowledge of good nutrition.

The students learned to sew and so much more. The pages of the *Angelicus*, the Barry College newspaper of the period, are laced with sketches of stunning original student designs—and not only designs for dresses, but hats and shoes as well.

Eat the
RIGHT FOODS DAILY
For Good Nutrition

MEAT
EGGS
MILK
POTATOES
VEGETABLES
FATS & SWEETS

Shades of the five musketeers! These students were not only avid fencing pupils, they were officers of the Recreational Athletic Association, an active group on campus organized to develop each member's social, moral, and physical potential. R.A.A. also put on Olympics Day. From left: Sandra Southmayd '63, vice president; Joyce Horacek '61, treasurer; Martha Saconchik, BA '61, MS '68, president; Rose Pillalha, social chairperson; and Martha Schurandt, secretary.

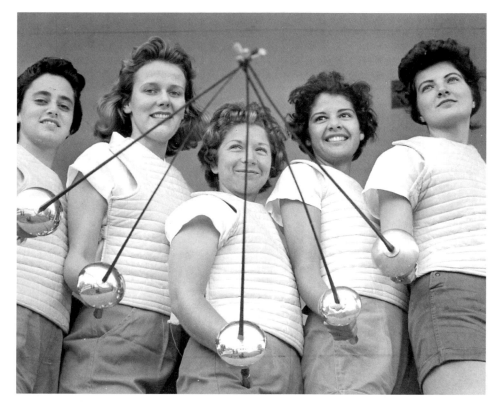

A mannequin can be an invaluable aid in achieving a proper fit, as this student learned in her dress-making class.

By 1965 when alums Mrs. James Mann of Albany, Georgia (left), Mrs. Walter Callahan of Miami (center), and Mrs. Cheatham Hodges of West Palm Beach (right), returned for a reunion, they studied a loom newly acquired for the home economics class and agreed equipment had improved.

Posing at Penafort Pool was a nice way to spend a free hour or two, even though there were no young men on campus in the early 1950s to appreciate the charm and grace of these students.

Swimming class in physical education was not only important, but enjoyable—especially when compared to calisthenics. These swimmers, however, were preparing to compete in the water ballet division on Olympics Day.

Archery was not only fun, it helped students develop upper-body strength, balance, and concentration.

Olympics Day was a treat for many of the regular routines were set aside as the classes vied against one another. The final scores were based on display of class banners, water ballet, sportsmanship, individual sports, and attendance records. Individual sports included basketball, baseball, tennis, archery, ping pong, and jacks. In this photo taken in the 1960s, Sister Nadine Foley, OP, oversaw a heated game of shuffleboard.

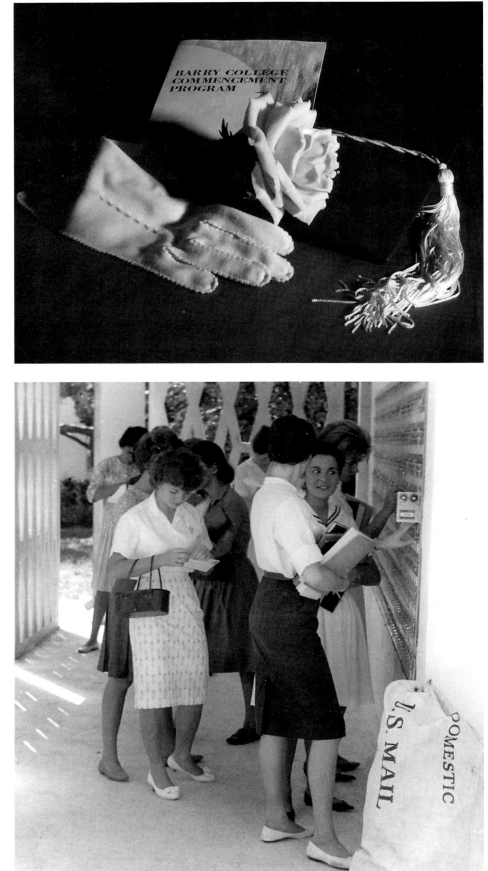

The way we were. Photographed for the 1966 commencement, the commencement program, mortarboard, white gloves, and roses were symbols of a way of life which was ending even as our country struggled to adapt to the social changes created by the turbulent '60s.

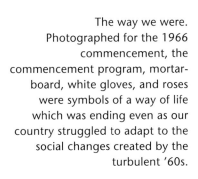

James Brennan, Father John Monroe, OP, Sister Mary Alice Collins, OP, executive vice president, U.S. Rep. Claude Pepper, and Father Louis O'Leary, OP, convened for a luncheon meeting at Thompson Hall to discuss the Post Office in April of 1963. Convincing the Federal Government to establish a station on campus and negotiating the necessary contracts was a complicated and time-consuming process.

One of the highlights of a Barry student's day was the walk to the campus Post Office to retrieve her mail. In part, the Post Office, which opened July 16, 1963, was due to the intervention of U.S. Congressman Claude Pepper of Miami. Rep. Pepper was one of Florida's most beloved statesmen and when asked to help Barry get a Post Office, he agreed.

Campus Queen Raquel Rivera '55, a native of Caguas, Puerto Rico, held court during her coronation on November 6, 1954. The title was not merely an indicator of personal popularity. A prominent college figure, the queen represented an all-around student and was noted for her spiritual values, character, scholarship, and leadership.

LEFT: The annual welcoming tea for freshmen was an exciting tradition as the new students began to form the friendships with the Sisters and other students that, in many instances, would last a lifetime. This tea was held September 14, 1958.

Taken on graduation day June 3, 1959, this photo shows Sister Trinita Flood bidding a fond farewell to Cabeth Caven '59 and Helen Grady '59. Graduation day inevitably arrived and inevitably roused mixed feelings of loss, finality, and nostalgia along with excitement and anticipation.

The eighteenth Annual Pan American Day celebration held April 11, 1960 followed the long-standing tradition of providing programs designed to improve inter-American relations. Students from the Latin countries carried their respective flags and acted as hostesses during the brunch which followed the Mass. Latin American students who participated were (clockwise, beginning left): Escarlet Pulido (holding the guitar), Nydia Torregrosa, Norma Gallegos, Anna Knohr, and Lillian Abudo.

In the 1950s, meeting proper young men was a very acceptable goal for college women—including these Barry students—and where better to meet them than at a college mixer?

Pan American Day at Barry College commenced with Mass followed by a day and evening filled with activities honoring our Pan American neighbors. In this photo taken April 18, 1955, Reverend Monsignor William Barry, rector of St. Patrick's Church of Miami Beach (fourth from left) followed the procession from the chapel of twenty-one Pan American flags. He is flanked on the left by Father John Monroe, OP, and Father Maurice Kissane. To his right are Father Louis O'Leary, OP, and, in the background, Sister Loyola Vath, OP.

Barry College's annual Baccalaureate Sunday began with the Holy Sacrifice of the Mass in the morning and concluded with the Rose and Candle ceremony (shown here, Class of 1957) in the evening. The Rose and Candle was one of Barry's most cherished traditions. Students marched onto the lawn of the fine arts quadrangle. Each junior carried a rose signifying friendship and each senior carried a candle representing knowledge. The juniors and seniors exchanged tokens while the rest of the student body sang "God Touched This Rose" and "Fare ye well, O Halls of Barry."

Although the BC on the freshman beanie worn by Gene Fitzpatrick could have stood for Barry College, it actually stood for Biscayne College, South Florida's first Catholic men's college opened in September 1962. Fitzpatrick was greeted by Barry student Mary Elizabeth Ballou '66. The Biscayne College freshmen were welcomed as official members of Barry College on October 21 and classroom facilities were made available to the Biscayne faculty until their new building was completed at 16400 Northwest 32nd Avenue.

This parade of Biscayne freshmen brought a startling new look to Barry campus as they proceeded to class, passing in front of Cor Jesu Chapel.

November 14, 1956 was a special day for John Graves Thompson, cofounder of Barry College and former mayor of Miami Shores. Here John receives Barry College's Laudare Medal as his wife, Elizabeth, reads the proclamation.

The coveted Barry College Laudare Medal was designed and executed by Sister Mary Joseph, OP, head of the Art Department. It is conferred on persons who have supported and befriended Barry College. The medal bears three trumpets which symbolize praise; from the trumpets hang banners which bear the Barry College shield. The first recipients in 1956 were John Graves Thompson, college cofounder, and Gerald A. Barry, the architect who designed the original five buildings.

A highlight of 1958 was the visit of film star and comic Bob Hope who received an honorary degree—Doctor of Hilaritatis—and later took time to sign autographs for students, including Student Council president Gail Hargadon '58.

This large, well-appointed lounge in Thompson Hall was a splendid place to meet and talk with friends.

This photo was taken in October of 1954 while students knelt during exposition of the Blessed Sacrament at Forty Hours Devotion. Throughout the month of October, they attended Rosary services every evening.

A candlelight procession in Cor Jesu Chapel.

In this photo, about 1952, of the investiture of the freshman class, cap and gown clad students led the procession across campus.

Once inside the auditorium, the investiture ceremony, shown here in 1956, began. At the ceremony, the freshmen were invested with the caps and gowns they would wear for formal academic occasions throughout their college years.

Penafort Pool was always a popular place, even in the midst of a busy day. By 1956 when this photo was taken, the landscaping was mature and the grounds were lovely.

Students met to study in the school's first library, which was located on the second floor of the Rotunda and used until 1952.

The Adrian Dominican Sisters walked by two's across campus to Cor Jesu Chapel where they chanted Matins at 5 o'clock in the afternoon, as shown in this 1961 photograph.

In January 1961, freshly returned from the Christmas break, student Diane Balconis '62 (foreground) did research in Barry College's new library, which was much roomier than the first and made necessary by a burgeoning student population. Located at the north end of Adrian Hall, this addition was torn down to make room for Weigand Center. This library was in use until February 1968, when the Monsignor William Barry Memorial Library was completed.

All was in readiness for the dedication of the first five buildings on February 4, 1941. The pontifical thrones in the photo had been brought from Adrian, Michigan by the Board of Trustees, to be used by Archbishop Amleto Giovanni Cicognani, the Apostolic Delegate, and Bishop Joseph P. Hurley of St. Augustine.

The Dalton-Dunspaugh lobby in 1962 had just been finished. The girls found it a joy, for it was bright, airy, and cheerful as well as comfortable.

The Rotunda in Adrian Hall was sleek and elegant. It was also the scene of many an afternoon tea. The silver tea service was used and the home economics teacher presided.

When finished, the exterior of the Dalton-Dunspaugh dorm, built thanks to a gift from the Dalton-Dunspaugh Foundation, was charming and homelike, in keeping with the atmosphere of the campus.

In this photo taken on Founders' Day November 14, 1957, the resident students enjoyed a brunch in Calaroga Hall. The building is now known as LaVoie Hall and the dining room in this photo is now the President's Suite.

Dorm rooms in 1962 came equipped with all a student's necessities, including desks and room for the stuffed animals that have remained a perennial favorite of college girls regardless of the state or school.

In 1989, Dr. J. Patrick Lee, Vice President for Academic Affairs, was moved to investigate the charming pelican statue that graces the entrance to Barry College in front of the Registrar's Office. He shared his discoveries in an address at the opening faculty assembly that year. He explained that the sculptor was John Miedema, a young Dutchman who moved with his family from Holland to Canada and then Miami around 1934 during the depression. Although trained as an architect and sculptor, he had difficulty finding a job and worked on various Works Progress Administration projects around Dade County. His daughter, Dirkje (known to her friends as Edith because her name was so difficult to pronounce) played a violin and received a music scholarship, entering Barry College as a freshman on September 18, 1942. Shy and struggling with the English language when she enrolled, Dirkje blossomed by year's end. That was her only year at Barry, for her father moved the family to Providence, Rhode Island where he'd heard there was work. Before they left in the summer of 1943, he sculpted the pelican from an art stone composed of coral and cement he'd invented and presented it to Barry College. The statue was mounted on a pedestal and placed where it stands today. Dr. Lee found and telephoned Dirkje Miedema—now Mrs. Gordon Rook and living in San Francisco, California. When asked why her father had chosen a pelican, she replied without hesitation, "Because it represents self sacrifice." And she continued, "That's what the Sisters on the faculty and staff at Barry represented—self sacrifice and unselfish giving of themselves to their students."

Monsignor William Barry founded *The Florida Catholic* newspaper, Florida's first Catholic weekly publication. Seen here during a quiet moment, he scanned the current issue.

Dedication Day—February 4, 1941—was the culmination of many months of planning. The students from St. Patrick High School of Miami Beach and St. Anthony's High School of Fort Lauderdale attended wearing caps and gowns, as did the Barry students. The Knights of Columbus handled the parking, provided ushers and a guard of honor. The guest list, described the next day by the *Miami News* as "The greatest assemblage of Catholic Church dignitaries ever seen in Florida," included Archbishop Edward Mooney of Detroit, Archbishop Samuel Stritch of Chicago, Archbishop John Glennon of St. Louis, Archbishop Joseph Rummel of New Orleans and Archbishop John T. McNicholas of Cincinnati, Ohio, as well as the President of the National Council of Catholic Women, President Bowman Ashe of the University of Miami, representatives from the Association of American Colleges and Rollins College, Director of the Miami Hospital, Miami Postmaster, Miami City Clerk, and the Costa Rican Consul.

Sister Bendicta Marie Ledwidge

Mother Mary Gerald Barry

Sister Thomasine McDonnell

Sister Mary Andrew Nolan

Sister Magdalen Marie Weber

General Council
1939 – 1945

The General Council 1939–1945. The five sisters who constituted the General Council of the Adrian, Michigan Dominican sisters in 1940–41 also became the first Barry College Board of Trustees, following the custom of many women's religious orders who opened an institution of higher education. The prioress general was often chosen as chairperson of the board. Shown here are members of the Adrian Dominican Sisters' general council, 1939–45, who a year after their election became ex officio members of Barry College's first board of trustees. From left: Sister Andrew Nolan, OP, supervisor for schools in Michigan and Ohio; Sister Benedicta Marie Ledwidge, OP, dean at Siena Heights College; Mother Gerald Barry, prioress general of the Adrian Dominican sisters and chairperson of the board; Sister Thomasine McDonnell, OP, music teacher at St. Joseph Academy, Adrian; and Sister Magdalen Marie Weber, OP, faculty member at Siena Heights College.

A highlight of the 1947 school year was the appearance in concert of the Trapp Family Singers. Their appearance was also an excellent example of the talented performing artists brought in to entertain the students at Barry College.

Sister Gonzaga Greene, OP, was named to supervise construction of the first five buildings in 1939. She watched bulldozers clear the land, conferred with the architect, and learned to read architectural blueprints. Daily, although not a small woman, she climbed ladders, walked the scaffolds, and strode purposefully across the roof as she checked the quality and progress of the construction. When the building program was completed, she was named vice president of Barry College and served in that capacity until May 1946. One of the greatest successes of her career came during World War II. The student body had marked a 100 percent increase and numbered 122 in September 1943. Housing and the shortage of building materials were critical issues—nationwide as well as at Barry—and Sister Gonzaga, taking her faith firmly in hand and heart, traveled to Washington, D.C. where she appeared before the War Production Board. She convinced the group of war-weary politicos that construction of an additional dormitory was an absolute necessity and received approval for the construction of Stella Matutina (Morning Star), a large freshman dormitory. It was erected under her supervision in 1945. She died July 31, 1956.

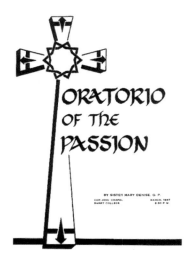

ORATORIO
OF THE
PASSION

BY SISTER MARY DENISE, O. P.
COR JESU CHAPEL   MARCH, 1947
BARRY COLLEGE   2:30 P.M.

Among Sister Denise's compositions was this "Oratorio Of The Passion" which was performed annually in March for a number of years. During World War II, Sister Denise played for more than five thousand servicemen at Opa Locka. She also had her own radio program on WIOD called "Piano Moods."

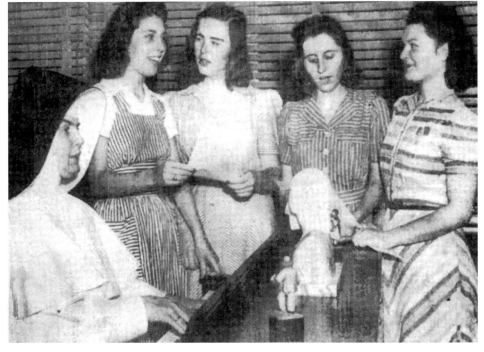

Sister Denise Mainville, OP, (left) was Barry's first music teacher and also a composer and librettist. The students rehearsing are (from left): Mary Jo Hackett, Detroit, Michigan; Estelle Geoghegan, Cincinnati, Ohio; Mary Jean Parez, Manitowoc, Wisconsin; and Mary Nell Alston, Clewiston, Florida. In 1941, Sister Denise formed the Tara Singers—modern counterparts of the minstrels who entertained in the ancient halls of Tara—and they not only performed for school events, but were very popular entertainers in the community. (Photo courtesy of the *Miami Herald*)

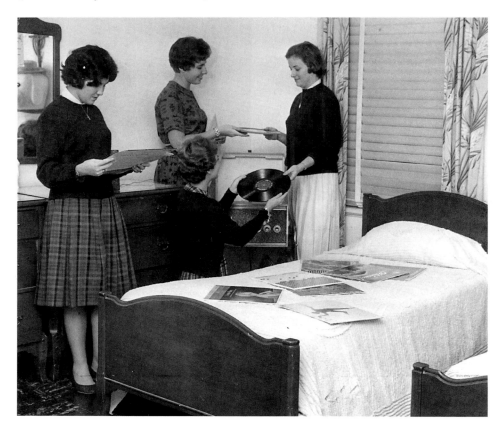

In the days before the omnipresent television set, these Barry students made sure they had space in their dorm room for their phonographs and record collections. Students discussing the merits of the different musicians in December 1960 were (from left): Susan Balduc, Barbara Begnalia, Ann McLoughlim, and Carol Bloom.

By September 1946, the new dormitory—Stella Matutina (now Weber Hall)—was home to that year's freshmen. According to "A Short History" published in 1961 and authored by Sister Mary Alice, OP, Executive Vice President, "The academic year of 1944–45 became known as the year of the great dispersal of the Villa. Seven houses were rented, located within two miles of the college . . . By the next year, the Gladmor Hotel at 74th and Biscayne was commandeered to annex another forty beds to Barry's elastic campus." The problems involved with supervising girls living off campus were multitudinous and everyone sighed with relief when Stella Matutina was cleared for occupancy.

Although in use since September of 1955, Barry's beautiful new Fine Arts Building and Auditorium were dedicated February 9, 1956 and blessed by Archbishop Joseph P. Hurley. The auditorium was a fully-equipped, 1,000-seat professional theater complete with state-of-the-art sound and lighting equipment. The building also contained a small lecture hall and a broadcasting booth with radio and television studios at the east end of the patio. The north section was devoted to music and drama with facilities for a small theater, classrooms, and practice rooms. The main building which was south of the patio included three large studios for ceramics, painting, and industrial arts. At the dedication, teachers and students gave demonstrations for visitors touring the buildings, but visitors were also able to view exhibits of graphic arts, ceramics, metalcraft, sculpture, and audio-visual presentations. It was a happy day for Mother Gerald Barry, OP, as she stood in front of the new building flanked by the Very Reverend William Marrin, OP, left, provincial; Archbishop Joseph P. Hurley of St. Augustine; and Archbishop Edward F. Hoban of Cleveland, Ohio.

The Barry shield or escutcheon is a combination of the arms of Bishop Patrick Barry and the Dominican Order. The white and black gyrons or triangles symbolize unity or the working together of a body of people for the common good. The cross with a fleur de lis at each end signifies victory, duty, and self-sacrifice. The sable or black signifies wisdom, silence, fortitude, and penance. The argent or silver symbolizes peace, purity, charity, and sincerity. The three red bars were taken from Bishop Barry's arms and the three shamrocks of his personal arms were dropped in favor of three books symbolizing a college. In creating the escutcheon for Barry College, the three books were moved to the right side or position of honor. The Dominican escutcheon forms the left side and indicates that Barry College is a Dominican foundation. In heraldry, as in stage setting, directions are reversed for the viewer. Therefore, the dexter, or right side of the shield, is the left side in this photo.

Very much in the spotlight was President John F. Kennedy as he appeared in Miami to attend a testimonial dinner at the Fontainebleau in 1962. The dinner, which honored President Kennedy, was a fund raiser for Senator George Smathers who was running for re-election. In the bottom photo, President Kennedy and Monsignor William Barry exchange greetings before Monsignor Barry gave the invocation. The two were old friends since the President and his family had often attended Sunday Mass at St. Patrick's on Miami Beach. Left to right attendees (above photo) included: U.S. Attorney General Richard Ervin (back row); Senator Jennings Randolph of West Virginia (front row); Julia (Mrs. Farris) Bryant; Thomas O'Malley, later Florida Treasurer (behind Smathers); Senator Smathers; President Kennedy; Congressman Dante Fascell; unidentified gentleman; Monsignor William Barry; Florida Treasurer J. Edwin Larson (back row behind Governor Bryant) and Florida Governor Farris Bryant.

The Florida Garden in the Fine Arts Quadrangle was one of the most beautiful and intriguing areas of the campus for it was landscaped with native flowers. The Starlight Ball was held in the garden until it was moved because of inclement weather several years in a row. Shown here is the North Portico of the Garden.

Sister Edmund Harrison, OP, left, executive vice president, Emily Edmunds, wife of Dr. J. Ollie Edmunds, president of Stetson University, and Sister Eulalia LaVoie, OP, head of the home and family department, pause near the cactus garden during a tour of the Barry campus on January 7, 1958. The Association of American Colleges was meeting that week in Miami Beach and the presidents' wives were invited to Barry for a coffee hour. Dr. Edmunds was president of the AAC in 1957-58.

Founders' Day November 20, 1962 was more memorable than usual because — in addition to honoring the founders of Barry College with a tribute of love, admiration, and prayer—three new buildings were dedicated. The procession led across campus where two new dormitories —Regina Caeli and Regina Mundi—were dedicated. And then the procession moved on to Thompson Hall, Barry College's Student Union, which was dedicated in memory of cofounder John Graves Thompson who had died in April 1962. A memorial plaque was to be installed in Thompson Hall honoring him and a plaque commemorating Mother Gerald's many years of service was to be erected in Cor Jesu Chapel. Conducting the requiem Mass had to be a bittersweet experience for Monsignor William Barry. He had previously bid farewell to his sister and brother and now he would miss his good friend John Thompson.

Sister Trinita Flood, OP, Board of Trustees chairperson Shepard Broad, and Archbishop Edward A. McCarthy shared a pleasant moment as they walked across campus on this Graduation Day in the mid 1970s. Recruited by cofounder Monsignor William Barry in 1966 to help the College expand its base by revising its Charter and bylaws, Shepard Broad was named to the Board of Trustees. In 1972, he was named chairperson. Barry University is now an independent institution governed by a self-perpetuating board of trustees, which includes at least five Adrian Dominican sisters. The Archbishop of Miami serves ex officio. When Shepard Broad stepped down, he became Chairman Emeritus. Under his leadership, many policy changes were initiated including the expansion of the Continuing Education program and initiation of the Miami Education Consortium. The Consortium made the business degree available to evening students and added a Bachelor of Science degree in Professional Studies. It also welcomed the community by offering adult seminar programs, workshops, non-credit courses, and received a grant for a project concerning "Crime Prevention for Older Adults."

CHAPTER TWO
Winds of Change

" . . . My Lord, when I heard the prayers in English . . . Wasn't that great, just great?
. . . We were singing as if it were a revival. A few people did, of course, complain,
'I like Latin better.'"
Excerpt from Et Cetera, a column by Naomi Davis
in which she wrote about the first Mass in English offered on campus.
December 16, 1964 issue of *Angelicus*, the student newspaper.

I n the fall of 1963, Sister Dorothy Browne, OP, was elected to serve as the first resident president of Barry College. Sadly, the excitement was short-lived for on November 22, 1963 President John F. Kennedy was assassinated. The American flag was flown at half-staff on the Barry College campus during the thirty-day period of mourning and a pall was cast over the usually joyous Christmas holidays.

Since 1940 the beautiful Rotunda of Adrian Hall has served a number of purposes. During the College's early years, the first floor housed a reception lounge. The second floor was the original library. Later the first floor housed the Admissions Office and the second floor was used as a classroom. In the 1990s the Registrar's Office was moved to the first floor while the administrative offices of the School of Natural and Health Sciences occupied the second floor.

The junior-senior prom in 1963 was an exciting event for Sally Kennedy and Steve Weiner as they paused to chat in the lounge.

Life continued, perhaps not as usual, but the Barry campus buzzed with activity as preparations were made for Sister Dorothy Browne's inauguration as president on February 5, 1964.

That same month a commentary in the *Angelicus* stirred debate on campus as the editor brought to light what she considered previously unmentionable topics, including the used book policy, exclusive consideration of Aristotelianism and Thomism, class attendance requirements, standards of dress (girls still weren't allowed to wear sleeveless dresses), the values of required retreat, sex and the Barry College girl. Of course, the fact that the editorial was published after having been read by the Sisters who were faculty advisors to the paper said something about the degree of editorial control. However, it also revealed the unrest that was surfacing not only at Barry, but also on college campuses around the nation. These comments spoke to the stirrings of the sexual revolution and women's liberation movement.

Sister Dorothy Browne's watch at the helm of Barry College would be marked by change . . . even the Sisters would have to adjust not only to liturgical changes, but even to the adoption of shorter habits. Latin, traditionally necessary to obtain

Cooperation and friendship were the order of the day as the Barry girls enjoyed studying and talking with the Biscayne freshmen in the lounge of Thompson Hall.

a bachelor of arts degree, was no longer a requirement. Barry College was beginning the transition from a small liberal arts institution to a comprehensive university offering bachelor's, master's, and doctoral degrees.

But not all of the change was disconcerting. As Barry marked its twenty-fifth anniversary on November 15, 1964, a ten-year development plan was unveiled that called for a $2 million memorial library to honor Monsignor William Barry, then the only living founder. It also included a $450,000 science building, $20,000 for tennis courts, $600,000 for a dormitory, $500,000 for a graduate school building, $425,000 for a school of social work, and a $750,000 scholarship endowment. Only two of these projects, the library and the science building, were undertaken, however. The library opened in 1967, and the Wiegand Center, which housed science laboratories, classrooms, and a language center, was completed in 1970.

Money was always very much on Sister Dorothy's mind, but it was a time when independent colleges everywhere were struggling. When Sister Eileen Rice, OP, interviewed Dr. Michael Connolly, a professor in the School of Social Work, he shared a special memory of one budget session several years before Sister Dorothy retired. "We looked at the budget and there seemed to be a $500,000 difference between the income and the outgo for the next year. She (Sister Dorothy) had said it was a balanced budget, but somebody said, 'Well, the figures still seem to imply that we're short on the income side.' There was a short pause, then Sister Dorothy replied, 'I assume by the end of the year I will collect that money, so it's balanced.'"

In 1967, for the first time, two lay members—Michael O'Neill and George Meister—were added to the Board of Trustees. This was significant because prior to this time officers of the Adrian Dominican congregation had functioned in an advisory capacity as trustees.

The wonders of the universe came clearly into focus via the lens of the new telescope, a recent gift. Seen on the roof of Thompson Hall are Suzanne Watters '66 and Judith Benkert, now an Adrian Dominican Sister.

Still another significant development was the formation of the Faculty Senate, which met for the first time on May 12, 1972 with Neill Miller, then Assistant Professor of Physical Education, as chairman. Prior to this, the Faculty Council, a less formally organized body, had served. The Faculty Senate was established as the organization through which the faculty would "formally and systematically participate in the governance of Barry College in accordance with the

As part of the program entitled "Experiment in Student Responsibility," Sister Arnold Benedetto, OP, academic dean (left), met with senior chemistry major Regina Grimek '65 and junior honor students Ofelita Schutte '66 and Margarita de la Liera.

In 1964, Sister Kenneth Duwelius, OP, the first religious to teach in a secular Florida university, taught English to Spanish-speaking physicians and surgeons who were enrolled in post-graduate studies at the University of Miami School of Medicine. Since 1960 Sister Kenneth, chairperson of the Spanish department at Barry College, had been offering extensive English language programs for Cuban and Latin American physicians, dentists, and lawyers, preparing them for board examinations in the United States, In the photo she is shown with Dr. Ines Olaya, an internist from Colombia; Dr. Segismundo Obregon, a pathologist from Cuba; and Dr. Mauricio Shitter, a surgeon from Argentina.

Before it was "politically correct" to be "politically correct," Barry College was just that. U.S. Senator Robert Dole, Republican from Kansas and chairman of the Republican National Committee, was the keynote speaker at the second annual president's dinner in 1972 while . . .

. . . in 1971, the guest speaker had been former U.S. Vice President Hubert H. Humphrey, Democrat from Minnesota. This photo, however, was taken during an earlier visit to Barry College in 1970 when he paused to be interviewed by a student journalist.

standards set forth by the Southern Association of Colleges and Schools and the American Association of University Professors." While the Faculty Senate's participation was advisory, it provided a forum to assess university policy and academic issues as well as an instrument for continued evaluation.

The years ahead would not be easy. In August of 1972, Miami Beach was the site of the Republican National Convention and, for the first time since World War II, the streets were lined with armed National Guardsmen brought in by the truckloads to keep the peace as demonstrators protested the Vietnam War. Although Barry College was never threatened by the demonstrations, the emotional impact was felt on campus. Yet when Barry began the fall semester a few weeks later, a total of 1,365 students enrolled, including a whopping 94 percent increase in the graduate School of Social Work. This was all the more remarkable because, in general, enrollment in independent colleges was dwindling.

In February of 1973, after twenty-five years of service to Barry College, Sister Dorothy Browne tendered her resignation effective June 1974, writing, "I think this great institution will be moved forward more effectively by a younger person, well-qualified to direct the Barry College community as we strive in new ways to attain the ideals our Founders held in their vision."

Sister Dorothy Browne had quietly, firmly guided Barry College safely through years filled with tumult and now the search was on for her successor.

This 1972 English class was held on the second floor of the versatile Rotunda. The instructor was Dr. Richard Mottram. The wall murals were a special point of pride because they had been done by Barry students—Stephanie Swiniuch and Bernice Gagnon, both from the class of 1951.

Hundreds of friends, supporters, students, and clergy turned out on December 15, 1966 as ground was broken for the Monsignor William Barry Library. The library, first building of a ten-year development plan, was erected directly behind the chapel. It was to house 300,000 volumes and provide temporary offices for administration and staff as well as classrooms for the School of Social Work, which had been inaugurated the previous September. From left: Monsignor James Enright, pastor of St. Rose of Lima parish; Edwin L. Wiegand, member of the Lay Advisory Board; Monsignor William Barry; and Michael O'Neill, also a member of the Lay Advisory Board.

February 14, 1968 was moving day. Three hundred Barry students spent Valentine's Day in a labor of love. First, the books in the library at Adrian Hall were packed in boxes. Next, a colored tag was attached to each box corresponding to a shelf in the new library where the books were to be shelved. Then the army of three hundred determined young women loaded the 63,000 books in cars . . .

. . . and drove to the new library where they unloaded the boxes and carried them into the building . . .

. . . where they unloaded the tomes, stored them on the appropriate shelves and . . . collapsed after a tough job well done! Sadly, Monsignor Barry had died the previous November without seeing the completed building. The Monsignor William Barry Memorial Library was dedicated on March 13, 1968. Ralph Renick, news anchor and vice president in charge of news at WTVJ-TV, Miami's Channel 4, was the chairman of the auditorium program. Reverend Robert J. Gannon, SJ, president emeritus of Fordham University, gave the keynote address.

The new library was a beautiful, welcoming sanctuary, a place where students could study and think and plan and, yes, dream—just as Monsignor Barry had envisioned.

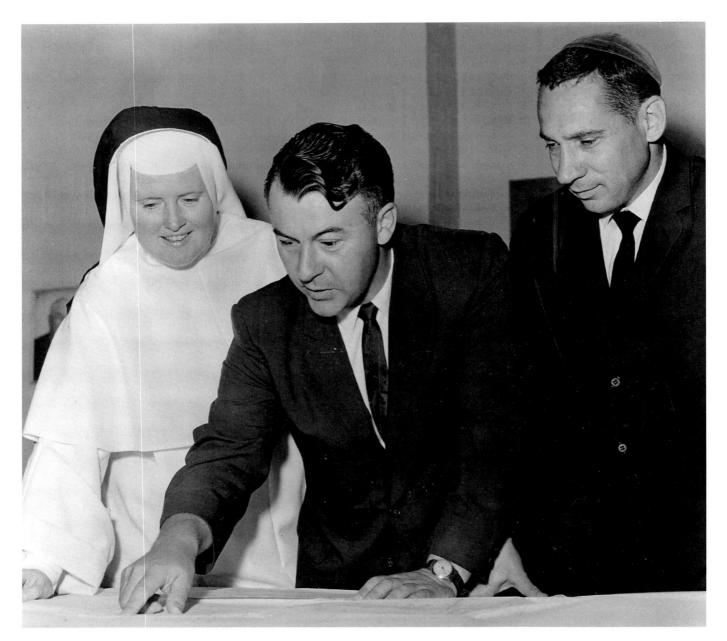

The School of Social Work opened in September 1966, marking the end of two years of work and planning that had begun in 1964 when the Dade County Welfare Planning Council called a meeting to report the shortage of social work personnel in the region. Since the nearest Master of Social Work program was 465 miles north at Florida State University in Tallahassee, there was no local source of trained social workers. Sister Dorothy Browne, OP, Barry president, stepped forward and, with the support of local agencies, immediately began working toward establishing a School of Social Work. In March of 1965, Dr. Henry McGinnis, formerly of Fordham University, was appointed dean. Thirty-three graduate students were admitted in the fall of 1966 and awarded twenty-three MSW degrees in May of 1968. The MSW program was accredited by the Council on Social Work Education in June of 1969 and has been continuously accredited since. A Ph.D. program in social work admitted its first students in 1982 and Barry University's first doctorates were awarded in May of 1986. In the photo, Sister Molly Lorms, OP, assistant professor and director of public relations for the School of Social Work, conferred with Dr. McGinnis (center) and Dr. Samuel Nadler, assistant professor of Social Work.

The 1961–62 season of the Barry Culture Series was rich with a diverse program of lectures, drama and musical events. Top notch entertainers ranging from the Preservation Hall Jazz Band of New Orleans . . .

. . . to the wholesome and upbeat New Christy Minstrels graced Barry's stage, as part of the series.

Sister Dorothy Browne wielded the shovel with great conviction at the groundbreaking of the Edwin L. Wiegand Science Building in the winter of 1968. The building was dedicated on March 18, 1970 in ceremonies highlighted by the presentation of the Laudare Medal to Wiegand, whose donation had made the building possible. The huge, 57,000 square-foot center contained a lecture hall, conference rooms, classrooms, offices, and science storage areas. From left: Edwin Wiegand; Sister Dorothy; Mother Genevieve Weber, OP, former president of Barry College (behind her); Father Cyril Burke, OP; and Michael O'Neill, member of the Board of Trustees.

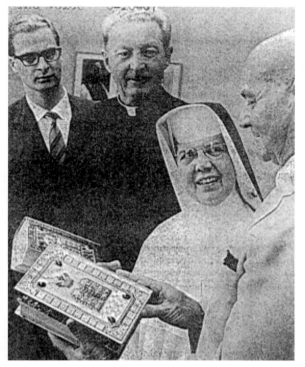

In appreciation for their role in the Catholic-Jewish Dialogue held at Barry College in December 1966, Monsignor James F. Enright and Sister Dorothy Browne received Jerusalem Bibles. From left: Arthur N. Teitelbaum, director, Florida Regional Office of the Anti-Defamation League; Monsignor Enright; Sister Dorothy; and Judge William Pallot, chairperson of the Florida Board of the League.

The Social Board kicked off the 1963 season with a hootenanny. Student talent performed with The Talismen, a versatile professional group that sang everything from folk ballads to blues. Barry's Latin American students sang the songs of their homelands, and after the music fest everyone enjoyed a marshmallow roast.

On December 22, 1972, Sister Dorothy Browne extended a congratulatory handshake to one of the first graduates of the Miami Education Consortium as he descended from the helicopter in Barry's "west 40"—a forty-acre tract of then undeveloped land west of North Miami Avenue. The Miami Education Consortium was established in 1971 as an association between Barry College and Embry-Riddle Aeronautical University to provide Miami residents who worked full time with the opportunity to complete college degree requirements. It was dissolved in 1984. To Sister Dorothy's left is Jack Hunt, then president of ERAU. On her right is M. Chapin Krech, director of the Consortium.

William Lev Litenatsky, the first Rabbi to graduate from Barry College, received congratulations from Monsignor William F. McKeever, diocesan superintendent of schools, and Sister Dorothy Browne. Asked why he chose Barry, Rabbi Litenatsky '67 said, "I heard about its high academic standards from friends. It's a unique college," he continued. "You're not just another cog in a wheel. The individual needs of the students are a major consideration."

Sister Dorothy Browne, OP, served as president from 1963 through 1974, steering Barry through one of the most tumultuous periods of the twentieth century. She was noted for a calm, caring demeanor that served Barry at a time of unrest in higher Catholic education in the United States. Sister Dorothy received her bachelor's degree from Siena Heights College and earned her master's and doctor's degrees from The Catholic University of America in Washington, D.C. She came to Barry in 1942 and headed the education department, then served as academic dean before becoming president. During her tenure, she served as chairperson of the Florida Independent Higher Educational Committee, secretary of the Independent Colleges and Universities of Florida, and became the first woman elected to be a fraternal delegate of the Southern Association of Colleges and Schools. She died in April 1997 at the age of ninety.

It was a solemn yet happy occasion when Sister Trinita Flood, OP, presented the very first Light of Flames Leadership Award to Don Shula (right), coach of the Miami Dolphins professional football team on March 11, 1977. The award was to be presented annually to honor a person "whose life has portrayed a belief in the teachings of the Judeo-Christian tradition which holds that morality must regulate the personal, family, economic, political and international life of mankind if civilization is to endure." The selection of Coach Shula as a role model was timely since Barry had been coeducational since 1975. Board of Trustees chairman Shepard Broad stood to Sister Trinita's right.

CHAPTER THREE
Of Barry Boys and Budgets

"Guys are big and they break things and put their feet where they're not supposed to . . ."
Dr. George Wanko, Vice President for Student Services
(Interviewed March 11, 1986 by Sister Eileen Rice, OP)

Once Sister Dorothy Browne tendered her resignation as president, the search for her successor was on. The Board of Trustees felt sure it would take time to find the right replacement for her, and Sister Trinita Flood, OP, then vice president of academic affairs, was named to head the search committee. Approaching her assignment with a spirit of diligence and determination, Sister Trinita secured applications from all across the country. However, time would soon reveal that the solution—the proper person—was closer than anyone suspected.

In the fall 1974 issue of the *Barry Mark*, Shepard Broad, then chairman of the Board of Trustees, wrote, "I began to receive a steady stream of communications, verbal and written, from the entire spectrum . . . including alumni, students, faculty, administrators and trustees, strongly urging the selection of Sister Trinita for the office of President." And so it was that on July 1, 1974 the search was ended and Sister Trinita Flood became the fourth president of Barry College.

The tumult of previous years calmed, but the currents of change, once unleashed, swept on. In the annual report covering her first year which she delivered on August 25, 1975 to the general assembly, she said, "Somehow and with God's help, all of us survived 1974-75 and here we are again to place another vote of confidence in each other to continue—and even to begin again—the work which is Barry College." It had

Further evidence of Barry College's involvement in the community is this award ceremony in which Barry trustee Ellen Whiteside McDonnell (left, standing next to Sister Trinita) and Sister Trinita were two of six women named "Florida Women of the '80s." The award was given by members of the Florida media and presented as part of the Elizabeth Arden Golf Classic held to benefit the American Cancer Society at Turnberry Isle Country Club on February 5, 1980. Also honored were then Dade County State Attorney Janet Reno, television newscaster Ann Bishop, and Barbara Weintraub. Also named was actor Suzanne Pleshette, not pictured. Reno, U.S. Attorney General as this book was written, has been a friend to Barry over the years. In 1978 she delivered the commencement address and, in 1993, she again gave the commencement address and received an honorary degree.

Paralyzed from a neck injury incurred during a high school football game in 1971, Greg Stead was an inspiration to Barry faculty and students alike. With the help of his family and fellow students who provided duplicates of class notes or reviewed them orally, he maintained a good academic record. On test days, Stead was permitted to respond orally or, if that wasn't feasible, a brother or sister accompanied him to class to help by marking the test papers. His graduation in 1978 was the outward symbol of his determination, stamina, and courage and it was a proud moment for everyone when Sister Trinita presented him with his Bachelor of Science degree.

indeed been a busy year, but one filled with accomplishment. A major restructuring of the admissions office had been accomplished—the various admission functions were consolidated and an experienced dean of admissions was hired as well as a bilingual recruiter.

Another significant change was the academic restructuring from undergraduate and graduate divisions to schools by discipline. The School of Arts and Science had a new dean; the School of Social Work had been re-accredited; workloads had been shifted and entire departments had been physically moved. In her report, she alluded to the myriad changes when she continued, "In case you have need to locate the Vice President for Academic Affairs, the Faculty Senate Secretary or the President, please visit Thompson Hall, first floor. The entire Division of Development and College and Community Relations will be found on Thompson second floor."

This was also the first year of the Office of Continuing Education. The Faculty Senate revised papers on Leaves and Sabbaticals, Continuing Contracts and Reappointment, Grievance and Appeals, Promotion, and the Summer Faculty Program. The major academic reorganization revealed the need for a new interface

When the male students arrived, strict rules governing coed interaction were established. One rule provided that male students were not allowed to enter female dorms except during brief visitation hours every other weekend. Complying with coed policies, Donald Ladolcetta '77—one of the first male students—whistled the popular song "I Love How You Love Me" beneath his college sweetheart's window. His purpose was twofold—to express his affection and to make sure she got up in time for her early morning classes. His ploy worked. He and Patty Cheffer '78 were married after graduation and their story became part of Barry lore. This photo was taken at an Alumni Reunion as was the photo of Phil Tempkins (below).

Although they had previously enrolled in graduate schools, male undergraduate students were allowed to enroll at Barry College for the first time in 1975, breaking a tradition that spanned more than three decades. That first year, the boys were housed off campus, but in 1976 the Villa (formerly a motel and shown in this photo) was opened as a boys' dorm and housed fifteen students. The Villa was conveniently located on NE Second Avenue across from the main campus.

The adjustment to males on campus wasn't always easy, as Phil Tempkins '76 learned. When Tempkins and two of his male colleagues decided to go for a swim in Barry's pool, they had to obtain notes from administration to prove to the security guards they were indeed Barry students. Even so, the hours they could use the pool were restricted and male students with long hair were required to wear swimming caps like the girls.

Class was business as usual. Male or female, they had to pay attention and they had to study.

between the deans and their faculties with the Offices of Admissions, Financial Aid, Registrar, and the Dean of Student Affairs. Another area strongly affected was Student Affairs. While previously the department had dealt almost exclusively with full-time undergraduate students, now services were to be extended to all—undergraduate and graduate, full and part time.

Nor was the physical plant neglected. Nearly four thousand maintenance requests were completed during Sister Trinita's first year as president. These included painting the exteriors of the chapel and auditorium and the interiors of Weber, Kelley, and Farrell Halls; renovating music department practice rooms and classrooms in Adrian Hall; servicing and repairing various air conditioning units; and bringing some of the older buildings up to the fire code. About two-thirds of the way into her address that memorable day, Sister Trinita said quietly, "This latter committee (Planning) is charged with looking again at the question of coeducation and reporting to the Board in October."

Not quite two months later on October 17, 1975, it became official.

The Board of Trustees voted to admit males to all undergraduate departments. Men had been accepted into graduate programs since 1954, but now—after thirty-five years—Barry was truly coeducational.

It would be a while before the male presence on campus was strongly felt. In an article headlined "Men At Barry" that appeared in the December 16, 1976 edition of *Hourglass*, the student newspaper, reporter Barbara Murphy mentioned that sixteen male students were living on campus. Not that they were necessarily quiet. One lone voice had been heard in the November 23, 1976 *Hourglass* when one of the "Barry Boys" took issue with the inscription "Barry College for Women" that appeared on the pillars marking the entrance to the school. For the most part, however, while disconcerted by the paucity of athletic programs for men, few complained about the student population ratio and were smoothly subsumed.

In February of 1978, Barry College launched a $12 million endowment and capital funds campaign. This represented a drastic departure from custom. In earlier years, approximately 60 percent of the college's operating budget had been derived from tuition and fees paid by the students. The contributed salaries of the Adrian Dominican Sisters accounted for six percent and two percent were realized from activities related to education. Gifts and grants had accounted for 15 percent

The picture below might well have represented the changing of the guard. Shepard Broad resigned as chairperson of the Board of Trustees at its annual meeting on May 20, 1977. He had served in that capacity since 1972. At the same meeting, Mrs. Inez Andreas (right) was elected chairperson to fill the position he had vacated. Mrs. Andreas received her master's degree from Barry in 1975. Following that and upon Sister Trinita Flood's urging, she became a member of the Board of Trustees. Mrs. Andreas continued as chair until 1996.

Because "His commitment to the American principle that no one who is able should be denied the advantage of education has led him to exert positive leadership within the Florida House of Representatives and the Senate," State Senator Robert Graham, Democrat from Miami, received an honorary doctor of laws degree. Sister Trinita made the award at mid-year graduation in January 1977.

and 17 percent had come from public services such as the real estate program, rental of facilities, and other special projects.

In discussing the campaign, Sister Trinita said, " . . . a successful campaign will assure greater stability for the college at a critical time in its history. It will also provide much needed support for our instructional program, and enable us to rejuvenate our original buildings for longer life and service."

It was a crucial step, for Barry's fortunes echoed the nation's and times were difficult. As the country labored under double-digit inflation, the savings and loan failures, and the lowest Dow Jones average in years, so Barry labored, struggling always to cut back—on everything but the quality of the education and the services provided for the students—to save, to reduce a deficit or to balance a budget.

In May 1980, after serving Barry College in various capacities for more than twenty years, Sister Trinita resigned as president effective July 1, 1981. In resigning, she said, " . . . the decade ahead will need a new vision and a new vigor and I believe these will come to Barry through new leadership." Her words would prove stunningly prescient.

The three tile panels at the entrance to the Edwin L. Wiegand Science Center were designed, made, and installed by art students under the direction of Regi Yanich, adjunct professor of art, and Sister Mary Joseph Kennedy, OP.

In October 1976, Barry College began its thirty-seventh year with more than 1,700 students, the largest enrollment in its history. Equally noteworthy was the fact that 1976 was the first year in which male students were housed on campus. The face of Barry was changing as was proven in this photo of an orientation week picnic.

"A Place of Peace" is how the November 1980 issue of the *Barry Mark* labeled the Botany Garden. The garden contained native trees, flowers, and plants which were nurtured by Mother Genevieve Weber, OP, and transplanted to various areas around campus. For many years, the cocktail party and reception held in late November or early December as part of the annual Starlight Ball, a major fundraiser, was held in the Botany Garden because it was so beautiful.

Sister Trinita Flood, OP, assumed her duties as the fourth president of Barry College on July 1, 1974. It was the culmination of years of dedication. She had first come to Barry in 1946 as an instructor of speech and drama and was vice president in charge of academic affairs at the time she was tapped to be president. M. Daniel Henry, vice president for academic affairs, is arranging her academic hood.

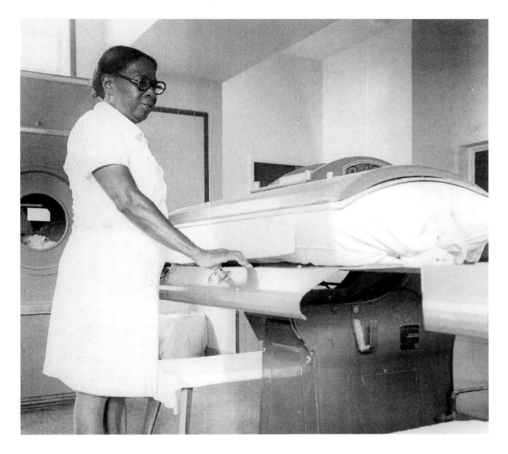

"I think it's time to rest," she said. "I'm ready to go fishing." Willie Mae Rogers deserved this rest when she retired in 1977 after thirty-three years of service in the laundry at Barry College. She is seen at the presser, where she ironed the sisters' long white habits as well as the linens used in the chapel and dining rooms.

Obadiah Gilley, groundskeeper, is shown pruning a tree he planted in 1953, a year and a half after he started working at the college at the age of nineteen. When he retired in 1996, Obadiah had spent his entire career in helping to create the serenity and beauty of Barry's campus.

The 13,500-square-foot classroom/office building that is currently under construction is north of the Fine Arts quadrangle and will face Northeast 115th Street. The first major gift of the public phase of Barry University's $100 million capital campaign—given by art collector and philanthropist B. Landon—will go toward its construction. It's scheduled to be completed in the fall of 2000.

FACING PAGE: The new Student Union Complex, named for R. Kirk Landon, the vice chairman of the Barry University Board of Trustees and former chairman of the board of directors of American Bankers Insurance Group Inc., will face North Miami Avenue just east of the Health and Sports Center and is scheduled for completion in the fall of 2002. A 73,000-square-foot building built at an estimated cost of $10.9 million, it provides space for a cafeteria, bookstore, fitness center, and the following student services departments: Vice President for Student Services, Residential Life, Student Activities, Career & Counseling, Health Services, Intercultural Center, SGA, Disability Services, and seminar/meeting rooms.

CHAPTER FOUR
Decades of Enthusiasm, Excellence and Expansion

*"When Sister Jeanne came on board, I discovered I was
on a steamboat going 200 miles per hour."*
– Sister John Karen Frei, OP
Interviewed in 1996 for an Inside Barry University program honoring
Sister Jeanne O'Laughlin's 50 years as an Adrian Dominican Sister

November 13, 1981 was a momentous day on the Barry campus. Barry College officially became Barry University and Sister Jeanne O'Laughlin was installed as the school's fifth president and the first president of Barry University. Shepard Broad, chairman emeritus of the Barry University Board of Trustees, brought greetings and congratulations from U.S. President Ronald Reagan. Florida Governor Bob Graham proclaimed November 13 as Barry University Day.

Once the celebration ended, Sister Jeanne faced a daunting task. Through no fault of the previous presidents, she had inherited a campus with buildings that had served the students long and well but now needed repairs and renovation, a student body with a declining enrollment, and a university in debt. Working with

Barry's Executive Committee for the Administration: Front row, left to right: Executive Vice President Sr. Peggy Albert, OP, Ph.D.; President Sr. Jeanne O'Laughlin, OP, Ph.D.; Back row, left to right: Associate Vice President for Research Sr. John Karen Frei, OP, Ph.D.; Senior Vice President for Business and Finance Timothy Czerniec; Provost and Senior Vice President for Academic Affairs J. Patrick Lee, Ph.D.; Vice President for Student Services Michael Griffin, Ph.D.; and Vice President for Institutional Advancement William Fenton, Jr.

the Executive Committee of the Administration, she established impressive, ambitious goals:

- Improve faculty/staff morale.
- Probe religious issues of the time.
- Understand and live out values of the Judeo-Christian tradition.
- Expand Barry's commitment to Florida.
- Interpret Barry to various "publics."
- Raise the quality of student life.
- Increase cash flow.
- Provide adequate resources to support the mission.

It wasn't long at all, however, until it was obvious that Sister Jeanne was more than equal to the task. She proved to be a human dynamo. She was—and is— everywhere on campus. From the very beginning of her tenure, she was never too busy to stop and chat with students, always able to find the time and compassion to counsel troubled students, to be supportive and loving in her dealings with her faculty and staff, and always, always accessible to the community as well.

Sister Jeanne was committed to making employees and students live the Barry Mission. She devised the "midnight shakes" test. According to her theory, someone could steal into a Barry person's bedroom, shake that person awake and ask, "What is your mission?" Without referring to any notes, the drowsy victim would be able to sit right up and promptly respond with Barry University's mission.

The proper reply was, "Our mission is to give quality education, to keep a religious dimension, to serve the community and to provide a caring environment."

By the end of the 1981-82 school year, incredible progress had been made. Despite lower enrollment figures, employees had received a six percent raise; the ratio of students to faculty remained 14-to-1; and the deficit was eliminated for the first time in thirteen years. Barry even ended the year with a surplus in excess of $134,000.

When school opened again in September of 1982, enrollment had soared to 3,218—an increase of 50 percent over the previous September. Suddenly the goals set earlier no longer seemed so distant and difficult to attain.

In the Barry University President's Report of 1984—a mere three years later,

Graduation Day—May 8, 1983—was filled with excitement and elation. In addition to graduation ceremonies held in the James L. Knight Center during which Speaker of the U.S. House Thomas P. "Tip" O'Neill gave the commencement address, ground was broken for the Andreas Building. Manning the shovels from left: U.S. Congressman Claude Pepper and O'Neill. That December, Pepper gave the commencement address for mid-winter graduates.

A formidable team, Dwayne (left) and Inez Andreas (right) proved to be generous, dedicated, and hard-working supporters of both Sr. Jeanne (center) and Barry University. In 1975, Mrs. Andreas returned to school and in 1976 received her master's degree in education. Accidentally overhearing school administrators lamenting the fact that a speaker scheduled to appear that same night at a major fund raiser had cancelled, she volunteered her friend and houseguest Hubert H. Humphrey. A few years later while visiting in Brussels, she recruited former U.S. Secretary of State Henry Kissinger. Wherever she traveled with her husband, who was Chairman of the Board of Archer Daniels Midland, she told people about Barry University and solicited their donations and support. Under her leadership, Barry completed a $50 million capital campaign; assets grew from $12.7 million to $57.6 million; campus facilities more than doubled from sixteen to forty buildings; enrollment grew from 1,900 to 7,000; and faculty increased from 76 to 244.

the following accomplishments were listed:

With regard to the goal of assuring a religious dimension for students and the community, the number of professed religious and priests working at Barry had increased 61 percent; religious studies were required as part of every undergraduate degree program; a Master's Degree Program in Jewish Studies had been established; and a campus ministry team comprised of ministers, rabbis, sisters, and priests was introduced.

Additionally, student financial aid had been increased by 106 percent, faculty and staff salaries had been increased by 17.5 percent, bringing them more in line with other universities of similar size; a $550,000 sewage treatment facility had been installed. Barry had become a member of the National Collegiate Athletic Association, Division II; built a new outdoor athletic facility; and added a full-time athletic director, six coaches, and a trainer to the staff. And the $134,000 surplus had grown to $346,768.

An incredible, almost dizzying pace had been set. It was as if Barry University, like Rip Van Winkle, was awakening and stirring to life after a decades-long nap. In the 1984-85 year, three dormitories were renovated. The Andreas School of Business and a ninety-six-bed residence hall represented the first new construction on campus in fourteen years. Barry continued to operate in the black; the surplus was now $470,000 and the first phase of a capital campaign closed with more than $10,000,000 in pledges.

On Sunday, November 13, 1983, Barry Auditorium was renamed as the Shepard and Ruth K. Broad Center for the Performing Arts. Broad, a close friend of Monsignor William Barry, was a long-time Barry supporter and member of the Board of Trustees and active in his community as well. He was instrumental in developing Bay Harbor Islands and served as the town's mayor for twenty-six consecutive one-year terms at an annual salary of one dollar. Additionally, he proposed that a causeway be built to connect Bay Harbor to the mainland. The Broad Causeway, authorized by the Florida Legislature in 1947 and completed in 1951, was financed by a self-liquidating bond issue which left the title in the town's name and cost residents nothing. Msgr. Barry had recruited Broad not only because of his stellar character, but also because of his financial acumen and leadership skills.

In 1992, Dwayne and Inez Andreas donated the funds to renovate the fifty-one-year-old Cor Jesu Chapel in honor of their friends Tip and Mildred O'Neill. On hand for the event were, from left: Sister Jeanne, Sister Marie Joseph Barry, OP, Millie and Tip O'Neill, and Dwayne and Inez Andreas.

By the time Barry University marked its fiftieth anniversary in 1990, the ratio of faculty to students remained 14-to-1, but everything else had changed. Enrollment had soared from 1,750 in 1981 to 5,900. Undergraduate majors had doubled from 25 to 50. In 1981, Barry University had awarded 475 degrees and in 1990, the number awarded was 1,316. In 1981, there had been no doctoral candidates; in 1990, Barry University graduated 46. Buildings on campus had grown from 16 to 40 and the annual surplus now totaled $602,850.

The student body had changed, reflecting the changes in society. Barry University now served more international and minority students. Students were older and males accounted for 38 percent of the enrollment.

Not only was Barry University accomplishing its goal of diversity, it celebrated those wonderful differences with Potpourri, an exuberant exhibition of international cuisine, art, music, and talent. The students and faculty continued to serve the community following the example Sister Jeanne had set when she stepped forward to help 620 Haitian refugees detained behind the ten-foot high barbed wire fences of Krome camp. And when she reached out to free three young Chinese women who had been denied political asylum. The women had been detained in a single hotel room for fourteen months. A year later she rescued another young Chinese woman and her two-year-old daughter from deportation. During this period she moved out into the community. She became the first woman ever appointed to the Orange Bowl Committee. She brought nationwide

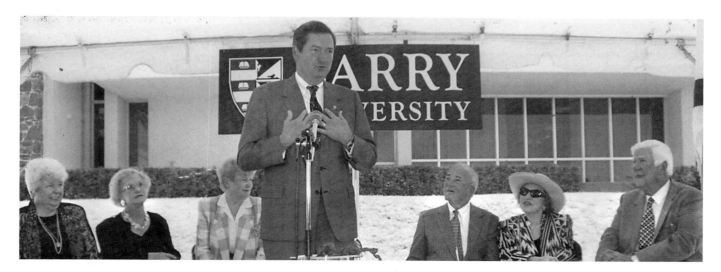

and favorable publicity to Barry University when she served as guest commentator for WSVN-Channel 7 coverage of Pope John Paul's visit and was profiled on the CBS Evening News in The Best People segment.

The students and faculty responded to her loving devotion. An interesting—and revealing—feature in the 1995 President's Report demonstrated how the students felt about their school.

"I was really touched by the Anointing of the Hands ceremony (held for Physical Therapy and Occupational Therapy Students). It made me feel that I'm going to leave Barry with the power to heal."

Oliva Olivero, Occupational Therapy Student

"I knew this was the right place for me the first time I visited from Nashville. I like coming to a Catholic University that teaches a sense of values and ethics. Sure, I miss home, but the way I look at it, I couldn't have come to a better place."

Matt Ryan, Freshman

And now, as this book is written in the spring of 2000, Barry University can look back on nearly two decades of unceasing progress since that November day in 1981 when Sister Jeanne O'Laughlin took a firm grasp on the president's gavel.

It's true that statistics don't tell the entire story. They don't begin to tell Sister Jeanne's story. They don't reveal the generosity of spirit, the courage, the humor she displayed when she met a benefactor's challenge and sang "Don't Cry For Me, Argentina" to ease a $1.5 million operational debt. Or her determination when she practiced for months so she could take a spin on the dance floor during the 1993 U.S. Ballroom Championships to raise $2 million for Barry.

Nor do statistics tell of the successes Barry alumni have made of their lives. Nor of the meaningful and selfless contributions the Barry students and faculty have made in our communities and our world. But statistics do speak to success and successful is an adjective that Barry can "wear" proudly.

In the past eighteen years, Barry's student body has grown from 1,750 to

U.S. Representative E. Clay Shaw paid tribute to his fellow legislator, U.S. Representative William Lehman, at the ground blessing on April 14, 1993 for the building named in Lehman's honor. From left: Sr. Grace Flowers, OP, Florida provincial of the Adrian Dominican Sisters; Inez Andreas, chairperson of the Barry University Board of Trustees; Sr. Jeanne O'Laughlin; Shaw; Lehman; Joan (Mrs. William) Lehman, sculptor and artist; and Tip O'Neill.

Garner Hall, named to honor James G. Garner whose charitable trust had supported the telecommunications program at Barry for many years, was dedicated in 1989. The 43-thousand square-foot building was paid for by a $3.92 million grant from Congress which was administered by the Federal Aviation Administration. It housed the School of Computer Science and the Department of Communication. The computer science section of the building contained three hundred personal computers. Two hundred were in an Ethernet Network and, along with twenty DEC terminals, were connected to a VAX 6310 mainframe computer and a UNIX network. As a result, Barry was able to offer students new computer and information technology courses as well as greater access to computers.

8,200—and it's still growing. Buildings now number forty-eight—with more under construction. The annual budget in the 1981-82 year was $8,361,461; in the 1998-99 year, it was $90,275,064. The number of people gainfully employed by Barry University has gone from 340 to 1,597. Total assets have multiplied from $15,955,019 to $89,269,250.

Through those years, Sister Jeanne's energy and enthusiasm have never flagged. During her golden anniversary as an Adrian Dominican Sister, interviewer Elizabeth Priore '98 asked about the source of her energy. Sister Jeanne replied, "I get my energy from the Lord, the students, my faculty and the excitement of who we can be and what we can do."

And, in addition to becoming a truly international center of learning, Barry University has not lost its loving heart. Under Sister Jeanne's aegis, Barry-funded scholarships and grants have increased from $500,514 to $18,816,101.

That would please the founders greatly.

They would be equally pleased to hear her say in her soft voice, "I . . . put the Institution (i.e., Barry University) in the hands of God."

Barry University and the school's future are truly in good hands.

Lehman Hall's main entrance faces North Miami Avenue. Rep. Lehman had a long association with Barry University and Sister Marie Carol Hurley, OP, who chaired his first campaign. Student aides from Barry served in his Washington office; his Congressional papers are deposited in the Barry Archives and Historical Collections. Professor Michael Melody of the Political Science Department at Barry was curator of the Congressman's papers from 1985 until they were placed in the Barry Archives in 1997 and also assisted him in writing the first draft of his memoir. In early 2000, Congressman Lehman published *Mr. Chairman: The Journal of a Congressional Appropriator*, an account of his twenty years in Congress.

ABOVE: Architects faced a daunting challenge in designing a building that met the needs of two schools—Education and Social Work. They created a two-winged, two-story building that houses dozens of offices, new classrooms including three computer labs, several common areas, and a large 200-seat classroom. The first floor houses the deans, classrooms, and public-access areas including a 400-foot student lounge. The second contains faculty and administrative offices. Facing north across a grassy savannah, the Samuel J. and Patsy Powers Building opened in the fall of 1994.

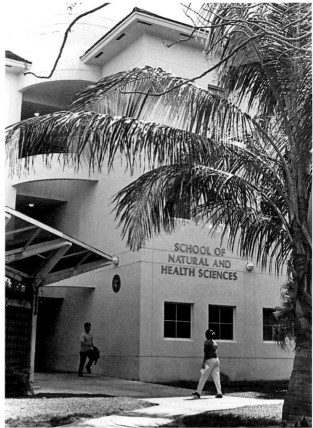

RIGHT: The School of Natural and Health Sciences was founded in 1991 and grew out of the Academic Health Science Center. Always dedicated to excellence, the Biology program has received a number of grants including the Minority Access to Research Careers and the Minority International Research Training Grant. As a result of these ongoing grants, Barry University has supported almost two hundred graduates, assisting with tuition or salaries as students advance to graduate and/or professional school. In 1990, Barry developed one of the first weekend programs in the nation to offer the Bachelor of Science degree in Occupational Therapy. Today a Master of Science degree is also offered. Acceptance to medical, dental, and veterinary schools throughout the nation is granted on first application to 90 percent of Barry undergraduates. Acceptance to medical school for Barry's biomedical science masters' graduates is 83 percent. Overall, Barry has graduated more than five hundred future doctors, dentists, and veterinarians.

Patsy Rooney Powers, shown here with Tom Powers, her stepson, was a loyal supporter of Barry University. Tom Powers, an alum who received both an MBA and an MS in Health Services Administration from Barry, currently serves as president of the Alumni Association. Mrs. Powers had given nearly $1 million in the memory of her late husband, Frank J. Rooney, for whom the Adult and Continuing Education School was named. Samuel J. Powers, her second husband, served as a trustee until his death on March 29, 1991. Noted for her generosity, Patsy Powers bequeathed $7 million to Barry. The Social Work/ Education building was built with funds from that bequest and named to honor the Powers family.

The groundbreaking for the $500,000, 11.75-acre sports complex on February 25, 1983 (not pictured) was the first new construction on Barry's campus in fifteen years and represented what Sr. Jeanne called "a sign of hope for the future." Her words proved prescient for the years ahead proved to be a period of unparalleled growth and expansion. Built on the back forty acres, the sports complex featured a 400-meter asphalt concrete running track that complied with National Collegiate Athletic Association specifications. The track's infield housed a soccer field. Two conventional softball fields, bleachers, and a building with restroom and storage facilities were also included. It would be followed by the construction of the $4.5 million Health and Sports Center (above) which houses the School of Human Performance and Leisure Sciences, in 1990.

The purpose of the Frank J. Rooney School of Adult and Continuing Education is to provide adult students with graduate and undergraduate credit, non-credit and certificate programs. Bachelor's degrees are offered in Professional Studies, Liberal Studies, Public Administration, Health Services Administration, Legal Studies, Information Technology, and Professional Administration. Classes are offered on the main campus as well as at thirteen off-campus sites throughout the state. Taking another positive step forward in the fall of 1998, ACE offered its first graduate degree—a Master of Science in Information Technology. The new program is designed for professionals with undergraduate degrees who are seeking leadership positions in the field of information technology. Classes are offered both in Miami and Orlando.

Eddie Colleti, director of athletics, displays a model of the proposed Health and Sports Center that made it easier to visualize what the center would look like and how it would function.

97

The Miami Shores-Barry University Connected Learning Community Charter School opened September 2, 1997 and was dedicated in December 1997. This photo was taken at the dedication. Operated as a private school with a customized curriculum although supported by tax dollars and grants, this is the second charter school in the area. In accord with Barry's philosophy of loving and celebrating diversity, the school has 180 sixth-grade students—one-third black, one-third Hispanic, one-third white. In addition to sharing land, facilities, and research data to keep the curriculum on the cutting edge, Barry interns and teaching assistants participate in the teaching teams. Parents also participate and in 1999 racked up almost five thousand volunteer hours. Students sign contracts with the school agreeing to be on time, to follow rules, and to get involved. A recent grant enabled students to collaborate with Barry's Schools of Nursing and Education along with Miami Shores health care professionals in hands-on science and health activities. In 1999, charter school students posted the third highest Stanford Achievement Test scores for middle schools in Miami-Dade County. At present, classes are conducted in six portables located on 115th Street, west of the tennis courts. The portables had been used by Miami Shores Elementary School students.

Ron Johnson '97, Barry's all-time leading scorer, dunked another two points for his team.

Barry continued developing its standard of athletic excellence in the spring of 2000 when the Buccaneer women's rowing team won its second consecutive Sunshine State Conference Championship in Tampa. From left: Leisl Jeffers '99, Alannah Miller, Ashley Birmingham, Christie Mendoza, Jenny Nilsson, Jenny Cox, Sonia Fajardo, Christine Riedinger, and coxswain Winonah Henry.

Decade of Success was the aptly chosen title for this photo of Coach Mike Covone (above, right) and his record as coach of Barry's women's soccer team (above) is proven by the statistics. The asterisks indicate the years they were national champs. Covone, current athletic director, revealed one of his success secrets in 1990 when Barry lost the match on overtime kicks during the semi-finals. Instead of berating the team or expressing his own frustration, he looked to the future, saying simply, "Spring training is coming up after vacation and we've got to work on several things. We'll see you then."

A DECADE OF SUCCESS

Year	Wins-Losses-Ties
1984	7-6-1
1985	12-2-2
1986	8-6-0
1987	13-3-1
1988	12-4-2
* 1989	17-0-1
1990	12-3-0
1991	11-3-1
* 1992	17-2-0
* 1993	17-1-0
1994	14-2-1
Total Record	140-32-9

* National champions

Barry University is very much at home and a part of its community. In this photo taken in July 1990, the Athletic Department continued that tradition by hosting a summer basketball camp for neighborhood youngsters.

ABOVE: As always, Barry moved forward to serve its neighbors and the community—in good times and bad. From the Campus Ministry office to the Maintenance Department, everyone pitched in. The Barry Hurricane Andrew Relief Fund and the daycare center were established. Sr. Jeanne led an interfaith prayer service broadcast live on WINZ radio and Barry opened its doors providing room and board to military personnel brought in to provide security and to assist in the rebuilding. Sr. Jeanne wrote President George Bush requesting assistance for the students and, within a few days, the President called to assure her the students would receive financial and disaster benefits. Shown here, Campus Minister Sr. Evie Storto, OP, directed Barry students as they filled hundreds of boxes with donated food for the hurricane victims.

FACING PAGE: Barry roared to life on October 18, 1996 as the sounds of construction trucks and earth-moving equipment invaded the peace and tranquility of the campus. It was the kick off of the Fall Beautification Project, launched by the Grounds Beautification Committee which called for the mass planting of 1,500 fully grown trees. The trees were a gift from Manuel Diaz of the Manuel Diaz Farms. Then 1,500 Barry supporters donated $100 each to cover the cost of transporting and planting the trees. Once planted, staff and students volunteered to be sure the palms were watered and tended. In this photo, Dr. Judith Balcerski and Herb Dunning were overseeing the planting of the trees which today provide a lush, tropical ambience to the campus.

Hurricane Andrew, which struck on August 24, 1992, was the most devastating storm to strike South Florida in eighty years. Nearly seventy people lost their lives and 45,000 homes were destroyed as a result of Andrew in Dade County alone. Mercifully, Barry University was spared with the exception of minor damage and the toppling of one of the largest trees on Barry's campus, located in the area between Weber Hall and Northeast Second Avenue. This ficus provided welcome shade from Florida's sometimes onerous sun.

Sr. Jeanne, shown here on the right, also served as co-chair of the We Will Rebuild Committee with Alvah H. Chapman, Jr. (left). Chapman was chief executive officer of Knight-Ridder newspapers which include the *Miami Herald*. The Committee, composed of civic, business, financial, and insurance leaders, raised money to hire construction managers to help rebuild in Andrew's aftermath.

In December 1994, U.S. President Bill Clinton focused national attention on Barry University when he was photographed and interviewed jogging while wearing a Barry shirt. The interviews appeared on CNN and various newspapers. The photo was so newsworthy, it was used as the cover of the very first *Barry Magazine* which was produced by University Relations and Enrollment Services. The *Barry Magazine* supplanted a previous publication—a tabloid newsletter named *The Flame*.

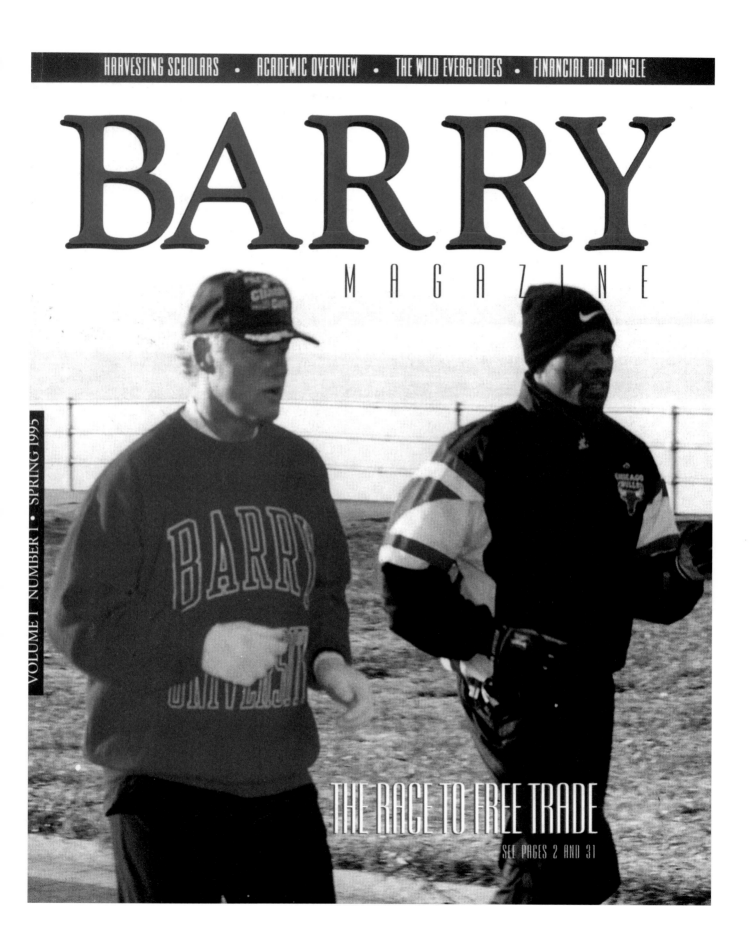

BARRY
MAGAZINE

VOLUME 1 · NUMBER 1 · SPRING 1995

THE RACE TO FREE TRADE
SEE PAGES 2 AND 31

This photo was taken at a steering committee meeting held in Miami prior to the Summit of the Americas which was hosted by President William Clinton in Miami on December 4–11, 1994. From left: Sister Jeanne O'Laughlin, First Lady Hillary Clinton, President Clinton, Board of Trustees Chair Inez Andreas, and Dwayne Andreas. At the time of the Summit, 20 percent of Barry's undergraduates attended on student visas; Barry offered an MBA on site in Jamaica and Sr. Jeanne made the comment, "Our commitment to the global community is strong."

David Brinkley (center) was on hand for the annual presentation of the David Brinkley Award for Excellence in Communication. He was joined by previous winners Bryan Norcross (1993), Ann Bishop (1990, second from left) and Ted Koppel (1995, far right) along with Inez Andreas, chair of the Barry University Board of Trustees.

Long before he was elected Florida's Governor, Jeb Bush gave Barry's commencement speech on May 10, 1992, which was also Mother's Day. It was his first such address and he confessed he had sought advice from his mother, former First Lady Barbara Bush. "She said to speak about 10 minutes, and that is what I intend to do," he said, also advising the graduates to realize learning does not end once you receive your diploma, to lead a successful family life, to cherish human connections that enrich our lives, and to stay active in the community.

Sister Jeanne O'Laughlin's inauguration on November 13, 1981 reunited four of Barry University's most revered and respected. From left: Former President Sr. Trinita Flood, OP (1974–1981); Current President Sr. Jeanne O'Laughlin, OP (1981 to present); Mother Genevieve Weber OP (acting president 1962–1963); and Former President Sr. Dorothy Browne, OP (1963–1974).

The late Senator J. William Fulbright (second from right), who secured federal funds to establish the prestigious Fulbright scholarship, visited Barry University in 1991 and posed for this photograph with four Barry Fulbright Scholars. From left: Provost and Senior Vice President Dr. J. Patrick Lee; Associate Dean of Arts and Sciences Dr. Linda Peterson; Associate Professor of Political Science Dr. George Cvejanovich; and Associate Professor of History Dr. Jesus Mendez.

On May 10, 1993, thousands of friends and relatives strained to see as Sr. Jeanne conferred honorary doctor of laws degrees upon long-time Barry friends United States Attorney General Janet Reno and former Congressman Dante B. Fascell. Fascell had served as a U.S. Congressman for thirty-eight years. President Clinton appointed Reno in 1992.

Sr. Jeanne O'Laughlin, OP, bestowed an honorary degree on Archbishop John C. Favalora on May 12, 1995 in recognition of "the spiritual leadership and depth of educational understanding he brings to the Archdiocese of Miami."

The 1985 graduating class had the honor of being Barry's then-largest graduating class as degrees were awarded to 872 students. During the ceremonies, Sr. Jeanne O'Laughlin (left) and Board of Trustees Vice Chair R. Kirk Landon (right) conferred an honorary doctor of laws degree on Marjorie Stoneman Douglas, author, Florida's first lady of conservation and environmental activist credited by many as being the woman who saved the Everglades. Also honored with an honorary doctor of laws was Alvah H. Chapman Jr.

Sr. Jeanne O'Laughlin (right) warmly welcomes R. Kirk Landon, co-vice chairman of the Board of Trustees, into the President's Circle at the 1999 Founders' Red, Black, and White Ball, in thanks for his $5 million gift toward the new student center building.

This was a special moment for Margarita Azurmendi '90. She came to the reception honoring Jaime Cardinal Ortega Alamino, Archbishop of Havana, held at Barry on May 28, 1995, because he was the priest who had officiated at her First Communion at the cathedral church of Matanzas, Cuba. Several hundred people attended the reception and the cardinal's earlier talk on the current state of the Catholic Church in Cuba.

Charles Modica, entrepreneur and educator, assumed the position of chair of the Barry University Board of Trustees in 1996. A resident of Jupiter Island, Florida, he got his start in business by co-investing in properties. He founded St. George's University School of Medicine in Grenada, British West Indies in 1977 and became its first and only chancellor. He got to know about Barry University's science offerings after the United States invasion of Grenada in October 1983, when he had to evacuate all of St. George's 560 students. He scrambled to arrange classes for students at schools in New York, New Jersey, and at Barry where he had recently joined the board of trustees. Today he sees Barry gaining more national recognition. "We've established a good history in a relatively short period of time as an institution," he says. "As our status increases as a Catholic university, I think Barry will become a significant player in higher education in the next decade or two."

Bishop Augustin Roman of the Miami Archdiocese offered the Mass on the Mall on Founders Day celebrated November 12, 1983. He was assisted by Reverend Michael Burke, OP. Bishop Roman, who had been expelled from Cuba in 1961 by Fidel Castro, worked diligently to help Cuban immigrants detained in prisons by the INS. In January 1993, he led a group of Cuban Americans to the Notre Dame d'Haiti Catholic Church to show support of Haitians on a hunger strike at Krome Detention Center. He also publicly denounced the United States' policy of summarily returning Haitian refugees to their homeland.

Volunteering in the community remains an important part of Barry University's mission. In this photo, a Barry coed tutors two students from Gratigny Elementary School, located on North Miami Avenue, four blocks north of Barry University, in reading skills. Sponsored by the Campus Ministry, volunteers usually work with elementary students referred by their ESOL (English as Second Language) teachers. In addition to working one-on-one with pupils, volunteers keep journals on each child to document improvement and future needs.

BELOW: Steve Althouse and students from his photography class took a field trip to the Galapagos Islands where they honed their skills using island wildlife as models. Jody Kosack Althouse, his wife, was instructor for an on-site introductory course on the ecology and evolution of the Islands.

Barry students participate in the annual Hunger Clean Up. In addition to raising money for the poor both nationally and internationally, students go into the needier sections of Miami to help residents clean up. In this photo, members of the Hunger Clean Up Core Team worked with children and residents in the Larchmont Gardens section in Little River, three miles south of Barry. Students plant shrubs or trees, paint, and clean yards or streets. In 1988, more than ninety students and faculty members worked with residents and raised more than $2,000.

It was a happy day for the twenty-six members of the Graham family who drove down from Deerfield Beach and beyond to attend Ada Graham's graduation from the Adult and Continuing Education (ACE) program in June 1992. Her graduation was another of the thousands of success stories adult students have added to ACE's annals since its inception in 1974.

Grants have enabled the School of Education to broaden its mission and serve larger populations. Three have been very significant: Project Infusion which provided teachers, through the "train the trainer" model, with education for technology infusion into the K-12 curriculum; the Migrant Education Consortium for Higher Achievement (MECHA) Project which provides education to traveling migrant children via videoconferencing and through the Internet online with WebTV; and the Deaver Grant Project which developed a course to educate teachers on bringing the Internet into their classroom curriculum.

In photo at right, Dr. Kathryn Campbell, Associate Professor of Sport & Exercise Science, works with Lisa M. Navas (left), Head Coach of Women's Softball, in Barry's sports medicine facility which offers the most modern treatment modalities available. Barry's Bachelor of Science degree program in Sports Medicine—Athletic Training is one of the first two programs in the United States to receive national accreditation by the Commission on Accreditation of Allied Health Education Programs.

The Fine Arts Department encourages students to pursue excellence in all areas that develop their creativity including performance, make up, and all other segments of theatrical production.

Dr. Laura Mudd and student researchers Isabelle Simeus and Jason Deleon examine fetal rat cells in their study of Fetal Alcohol Syndrome. The research, conducted by Dr. Mudd and Dr. Jeremy Montague and published in the *McGill Journal of Medicine*, demonstrates that when estrogen and five growth factors are introduced simultaneously with alcohol, brain cell death caused by ethanol poisoning is reduced. These findings could possibly lead to treatment options for FAS mentally retarded babies.

The 35,000-square-foot building that houses both the education and social work schools was built with $2.6 million from Patsy Powers' $7 million bequest, the largest single gift in the school's then fifty-one-year history. A $4-million endowment fund was established with the balance.

Dr. Charles Southerland, DPM, (right) from the Barry University School of Graduate Medical Sciences, is shown treating a crippled child as part of the Yucatan Crippled Children's Project in July 1998. The project was organized as an outgrowth of a program of humanitarian relief to the Yucatan Peninsula established in 1988 after the area was devastated by Hurricane Gilbert. Dr. Southerland works with medical professionals and Mexican public officials to bring medical care to the crippled children as an ongoing project. On July 4, 1996, he first led a team of podiatric physicians to Merida where they performed surgery on disadvantaged children. He returns monthly and the lines of children waiting to see him and his medical team get longer and longer. During the first eighteen months of operation, the Project rendered treatment to more than 250 patients.

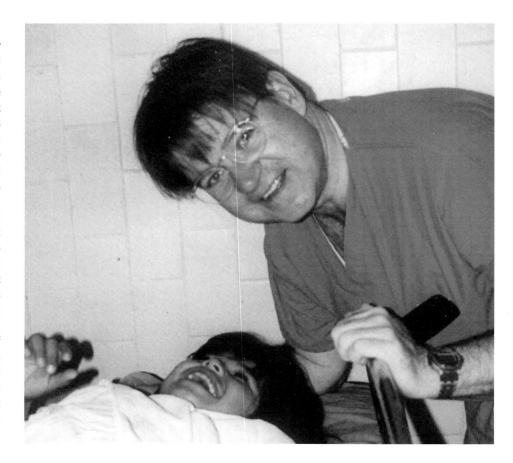

Assistant Nursing Professor Marcia Hacker provides health screening for students at Gratigny Elementary, one of six schools in Barry's Primary Care Nursing Center (PCNC). The PCNC at Barry University School of Nursing was established in 1993 to provide health care and education for students and their families and to evaluate the effectiveness of the Center's activities in the promotion of health for children and those who care for them. Since its inception, more than 24,000 student contact hours have been provided at the schools. Governor Jeb Bush appointed Hacker a member of his Alzheimer's Disease Advisory Committee in June 2000.

In this photo, taken in the kitchen of Sister Jeanne's Miami Beach home on the evening of April 12, 2000, Elián Gonzalez paused with his cousin Marisleysis Gonzalez and Sister Jeanne. The previous Thanksgiving, the six-year-old boy had fled from Cuba with his mother, who drowned in the attempt. After a brief hospitalization, he was released into the custody of his father's uncle Lazaro Gonzalez and other relatives living in Miami. The Cuban government sent a diplomatic note to the U.S. mission in Havana requesting return of the child to Cuba. His father, Juan Miguel Gonzalez, a Cuban national park employee, also wanted his son returned to Cuba. Elián's relatives in Little Havana filed a petition with Immigration and Naturalization Services requesting that Elián be given asylum in the United States. On April 22, 2000, the INS removed Elián from his great uncle Lazaro Gonzalez's home. Ultimately, the 11th Circuit Court of Appeals denied Elián an asylum hearing and he returned to Cuba with his father.

In the early 1980s, Sr. Jeanne received an urgent telephone call from Ucola Katzentine, a long-time friend and supporter of Barry University. Mrs. Katzentine was the widow of Frank Katzentine, mayor of Miami in 1930 and founder of WKAT radio in 1937. "If you want this house, get over here in 30 minutes," Mrs. Katzentine said. Sr. Jeanne complied and, as a result, this seven-bedroom, 6,957 square-foot home was bequeathed to Barry. There was one requirement: a university official must live in the Pine Tree Drive home for ten years. Following Mrs. Katzentine's death in 1986, the home—built in 1930 and valued in 1987 at $347,000—needed plaster and paint, plumbing and wiring. Sr. Jeanne moved into the home in March 1987 and has resided there since, utilizing the home as not only a residence, but as the backdrop for many meetings and receptions. As this book was written, the home served as the backdrop for an event of international significance—it was used as a neutral zone where Elián Gonzalez met with his grandmothers from Cuba.

In 1997, the Ford Foundation awarded Barry University a $50,000 grant to devise a plan that would help Catholic colleges and universities embrace and build upon their diversity. Barry has made diversity a high priority since the day its doors first opened sixty years ago. Today students from around the world come to Barry to learn and, in many instances, to return and take leadership roles in their native countries. On campus, a number of organizations welcome students from various cultures such as the Black Student Organization, the Jamaican Club, the International Council, the Haitian Intercultural Association, the Hispanic Association, and Women In Action. Barry's success is marked by the fact that it has been ranked number one for diversity among universities in the South by *U.S. News & World Report.*

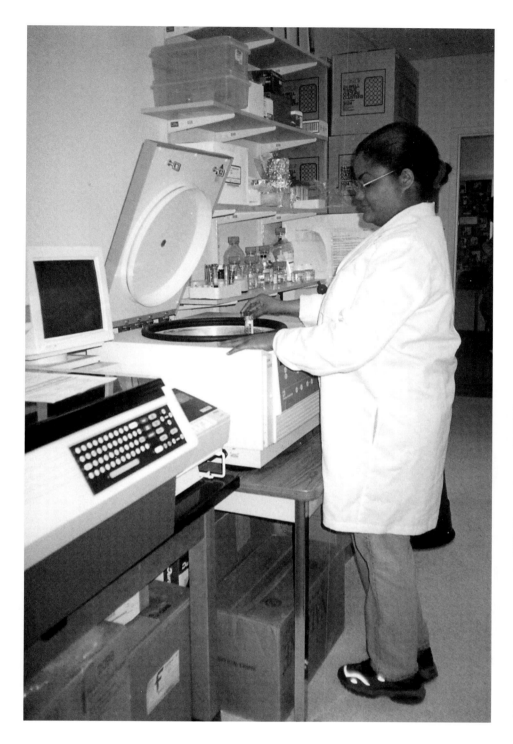

In this photo, MARC grant student Ria Achong works on an assignment in the Research Lab of the School of Natural and Health Sciences. MARC, an acronym for the Minority Access to Research Careers program, was launched at Barry in the fall of 1983 when the school first received a MARC grant from the National Institutes of Health. The grant was established to prepare minority students to compete successfully for places in graduate school programs leading to a Ph.D. in the biomedical sciences. The program has been so successful that the number of the grants increased over the years making the program accessible to an ever-increasing number of talented minority students.

Dr. George Wanko warmly congratulates Arleen Dowd, winner of the 1980 St. Katherine's Medal. Dr. Wanko served as dean of students from 1978 to 1981, then as vice president for student affairs (later renamed student services) until his untimely death in 1999. Affectionately known simply as "Doc," he welcomed twenty-two incoming classes at Barry.

FACING PAGE: On May 8, 1983, Inez Andreas hoisted the first shovelful of earth at the groundbreaking for the D. Inez Andreas School of Business. The building was opened for classes in September 1984 and her friend Henry Kissinger attended the building's dedication on February 24, 1985. When this photo was taken, the building had been readied for the dedication.

Because of Barry's religious heritage and foundation, the school is interested in helping students grow spiritually as well as academically. In this photo, Reverend Mark Wedig, OP, chair of the Theology Department, pauses to chat with a student.

Photographed January 24, 2000 at the dedication of the new Center for Excellence in Learning and Teaching (CELT) were Associate Vice President and Dean for Information Technology John Beaubrun, Director of Library Services Nancy Maxwell, Barry President Sr. Jeanne O'Laughlin, and Associate Dean of the Division of Information Technology Dr. Cynthia Davis. CELT is an instructional facility located in the library and equipped with fifteen computers, printers, projector, and teleconferencing equipment. The facility is designed for faculty workshops and group sessions. It also contains a smaller area where faculty members can work on individual projects. Funded by a Title III grant from the U.S. Department of Education, the purpose of CELT is to assist the faculty to incorporate new computer and video-based technologies into their teaching and instructional activities.

From the outset, the School of Social Work distinguished itself with an emphasis on a hands-on, nuts and bolts approach to social work practice which helps people solve their problems. Barry's emphasis is in the training of highly skilled professionals who are effective in assisting their clients to improve the quality of their lives. The focus at Barry is clinical. Students in the Master of Social Work program spend as much or more time in closely supervised work at social work agencies as in the classroom. The School's goal is not merely to study social work theory, but to actually make a difference in people's lives. The School has continued to serve the needs of South Florida's diverse population and to respond to newly emerging social problems such as homelessness, AIDS, family violence, and substance abuse.

Anna Halbergson '00—shown here at the 2000 athletic banquet with Dr. Jean Cerra, vice provost for enrollment and academic services and dean, School of Human Performance and Leisure Sciences, and Dr. J. Patrick Lee, provost/senior vice president for academic affairs—has won the prestigious National Collegiate Athletic Association's Walter Byers Postgraduate Scholarship making Barry University the first institution ever to boast two recipients of the award. Halbergson is captain of the women's tennis team and a biology major with a 4.0 GPA. Marya Morusiewicz, co-captain of the 1995 women's national champion volleyball team and a sports medicine-athletic training major with a 4.0 GPA, won in 1997. Marya used the $10,000 award to attend the University of Miami where she received a master of science degree in physical therapy in December 1999. The Byers Award is given annually to one male and one female student athlete in recognition of outstanding academic achievement in any of the NCAA Division I, II, and III schools. On June 12, 2000, Dr. Cerra was inducted into the National Association of Collegiate Directors of Athletics Hall of Fame at special ceremonies in Orlando, Florida.

The Barry license tag, now available to drivers who wish to show their pride and support of Barry University, was the result of a great deal of work. Florida Representative Beryl Roberts-Burke sponsored the bill authorizing the license plates in the House and Senator Howard C. Furman introduced it in the Senate. MBNA gave the University a $30,000 advance against expected royalties from the alumni card for the application fee. The most grueling task was obtaining 10,000 signatures from licensed Florida drivers supporting issuance of the plate. The Alumni Board, staff, and volunteers went above and beyond, collecting nearly 13,000 signatures, and the license plate became a reality.

CHAPTER FIVE
Through the Years

All hail to Barry—hail to Barry, Alma Mater proud and true.
Always caring—ever sharing, our heart longs to be with you.
Time could never dim the flame of memories that will remain.
We'll remember dear old Barry and smile when e'er we hear your name.
— Words and Music by Frank X. Loconto
Barry University Alma Mater

The colorful photos in this chapter represent the many facets of Barry University as it has grown in the past six decades from the small college that opened its doors with an enrollment of forty-five students to its present student population, which numbered more than eight thousand undergraduate and graduate students in the spring of 2000.

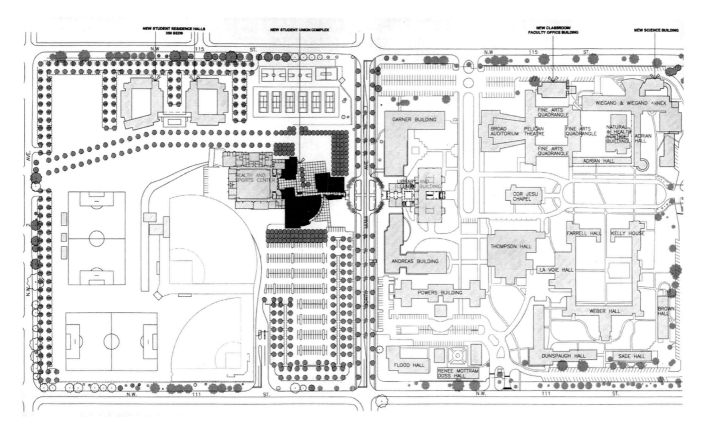

This schematic drawing of the Barry campus done in 1999 shows how dramatically the University has grown over the years. The schematic also pinpoints the new student residence halls (upper left) which will add 350 beds and the new R. Kirk Landon Student Center (in red), named for the vice chairman of the Barry University Board of Trustees, which will face North Miami Avenue just east of the Health and Sports Center. The classroom/office building will face Northeast 115 Street and is located at the upper right.

Important Dates In Barry's History

1939
- Purchase of Barry property (May)
- Sister Gonzaga Greene appointed as first administrator in November 1939 (1940–1946)

1940
- **Mother Gerald Barry becomes Co-founder and President (1940–1961)**
- Ground broken for campus buildings on January 24
- Charter for Barry College approved on February 5
- Bishop Patrick Barry, founder, dies on August 13
- Opening classes held on September 19
- *Barry College Digest*, first student newspaper, mimeographed
- Adrian Hall, Cor Jesu Chapel, Farrell Hall, Kelley House, and LaVoie Hall completed

Barry College had marked only eight years when this tinted photograph of the entrance was taken in 1948. In the center is Cor Jesu Chapel, a gift of Mrs. Margaret Brady Farrell, a winter resident and a member of Monsignor Barry's parish in Miami Beach. One of the original buildings, it has served as the spiritual heart of the campus since its construction.

1941
- Barry College dedicated on February 4
- First student retreat opened on April 6
- *Barry College Digest* renamed as *Angelicus*; first issue appears June 4
- First Honors Convocation held in Adrian Hall rotunda on June 5
- Completion of Penafort Pool on July 1
- First Conference on "Spiritual Pan Americanism" on December 31
- First Founders' Day celebrated on November 15

1942

- First Baccalaureate exercises on Sunday, May 31
- First Commencement: 10 women graduated on June 3

1943

- Provisional teaching certificates issued to qualified Barry students by Florida Department of Education established on March 5
- First Pan American Day on campus on March 14

1944

- First class rating given by Associated College Press to *Angelicus*

1945

- First constitution for student council approved by faculty on January 14
- Groundbreaking for Stella Matutina (now Weber Hall) on September 10

1946

- Sister Marie Grace Gibney appointed executive vice president (1946–1952)
- First installation of Student Council on October 13
- Completion of Weber Hall for September opening

1947

- First accreditation granted by Southern Association of Colleges and Schools

1952

- Sister Edmund Harrison appointed executive vice president (1952–1958)

1953

- Department of Nursing opened

The light streaming through the wrought iron doors leading into Cor Jesu was a welcome beacon to Barry's students. The doors, first installed in 1953, were removed in 1970 when the chapel was renovated.

Shown in this photo is the first Starlight Ball held December 9, 1978. One of Barry College's most successful fund and "friend" raising events, the black tie gala was noted for its beautiful decorations and breathtaking surroundings. The Starlight Ball Committee, comprised of students, faculty, and staff, supervised every detail of the evening which was a smashing success. Sister Trinita Flood, OP, greeted guests, Archbishop Edward McCarthy gave the Invocation, and the Barry Keynotes provided the musical entertainment. Later guests danced beneath twinkling lights to an eight-piece orchestra enjoying a picture perfect Miami night.

In this formal portrait of the Tara Singers taken in May 1963, the young women epitomized the femininity that had been the hallmark of the Barry student since its inception. The Tara Singers were founded by Sister Denise Mainville, OP, in the school's first year of existence.

1954
- Ground breaking for Auditorium and Fine Arts Quadrangle on July 29
- First graduate programs offered
- First capping of nursing students on January 13

1956
- Barry Villa purchased
- Master's degree conferred on first male student
- First master's degrees in education awarded on May 30

1958
- Sister Mary Alice Collins appointed as executive vice president (1958–1963)

1960
- Barry accepted as member of Association of Independent Colleges and Universities of Florida (ICUF)

1961
- Re-accreditation received from SACS
- Mother Gerald Barry, founder, dies

1962
- **Mother Genevieve Weber elected Prioress General and named second President of Barry College (1961–1963)**
- John Graves Thompson, founder, dies
- Nursing program accredited
- Dalton-Dunspaugh House and Thompson Hall completed

1963
- **Sister Dorothy Browne elected third President (1963–1974) of Barry College**
- Barry Post Office dedicated

The Adrian Dominican Sisters chanting the Latin Office of the Blessed Virgin in Cor Jesu Chapel in 1961.

1965
- *Barry Mark*, University Relations publication, introduced

1966
- Graduate School of Social Work opened

1967
- First lay members added to Board of Trustees
- Monsignor William Barry Library dedicated (March)
- Monsignor William Barry, founder, dies (November)

Barry's state-of-the-art television studio was named to honor David Brinkley, former NBC White House correspondent and co-anchor with Chet Huntley of the Huntley-Brinkley Report. In 1987, Brinkley was the first recipient of the Barry University Award for Excellence in Communication because of his more than forty years of distinguished service in the field of communication. In addition the award was renamed the "David Brinkley Award for Excellence in Communication." He also served as an adjunct professor in communication at Barry. As further emphasis was placed on communications, the Barry Channel debuted October 16, 1991 offering programs written, directed, and produced by students. The Communication Department made impressive strides when it held its first International Video-Conference with the Universita di Lecce in Lecce, Italy via a satellite dish provided by Tele-Link and a grant from Southern Bell.

1968
- School of Social Work accredited

1970
- Wiegand Science Center completed
- *Angelicus:* student newspaper title changed to *Hourglass*

1971
- Shepard Broad elected chair, Board of Trustees
- Re-accreditation by SACS

1974
- **Sister Trinita Flood elected fourth President (1974–1981) of Barry College**
- Long-range planning begun
- Schools of Education and Nursing, the Division of Fine Arts, and the Department of Continuing Education created, 1974–1975
- Graduate/Undergraduate structure changed to one oriented by academic disciplines

1975
- Admission of male students to all programs approved by Board of Trustees
- School of Arts and Sciences established

1977
- D. Inez Andreas elected chair, Board of Trustees

1978
- School of Business established
- Starlight Ball inaugurated; later renamed Founders' Ball

In 1991, Barry University hosted approximately two hundred volunteers with Habitat for Humanity. Sister Jeanne O'Laughlin, OP, and former U.S. President Jimmy Carter found time for conversation during the busy week.

1981

- **Sister Jeanne O'Laughlin elected fifth President (July 1981–present) of Barry College**
- Barry College becomes Barry University
- *Barry Mark* becomes *The Flame*
- Capital Campaign begun

1982

- Construction of D. Inez Andreas School of Business

1983

- Division of Biological and Biomedical Sciences established
- Frank J. Rooney School of Adult & Continuing Education building purchased
- Honors Program initiated

1984

- Sage (South) Hall completed
- Intercollegiate sports teams join NCAA Division II
- *Hourglass*, student newspaper, becomes *Buccaneer*

The acquisition of Barry's tenth school, the University of Orlando Law School, was announced on March 17, 1999 and marked still another step in Barry's growth and the fulfillment of Sister Jeanne O'Laughlin's eighteen-year dream. The law school, renamed Barry University School of Law, opened in 1995. It has remained at its location on East Colonial Drive in Orlando and graduated its first students in December 1999. "No woman religious-founded college has ever had a law school," said Sister Jeanne. "We're making history. Our goal is to develop a first class law school in Central Florida that will serve students from Tampa to Cocoa Beach and from Flagler to Palm Beach County." UO had two other degree programs—education and business. Barry processed the education students into its own program and UO retained responsibility for the business students.

Bucky Buccaneer, the colorful campus mascot, is ever present and represents the spirit of the teams.

Representatives from more than thirty nations demonstrated their colors during the April 19, 1999 Festival of Nations, which attracted 1,000-plus visitors to Barry's campus. The day featured cultural displays, food, and entertainment from around the world. The Intercultural Student Center sponsored the second annual observation of the event.

1985

- D. Inez Andreas School of Business building dedicated
- Browne (East) Hall completed
- School of Podiatric Medicine established (accreditation received in 1988)
- Academic Health Science Center established
- Rathskeller opened on campus (September)

1986

- Ph.D. program in social work initiated

1987

- Barry-St. Francis Foot Clinic opened (March)
- Flood (West) Hall completed

1988

- Brooks Petty and Annie Perez named Barry's first all-American athletes
- Michelle Fulton named Barry's first Truman Scholar
- Barry joins Sunshine State Conference (June)

1989

- LIFE Program started at Barry (June)
- Garner Hall dedicated (November)
- First National Collegiate Athletic Association-II championship won by women's soccer team (November)

1990

- Mottram Doss Residence hall dedicated (April)
- Health and Sports center dedicated (December)
- Alumni time capsule buried in Health and Sports center

1991

- School of Natural and Health Sciences established (May)
- Division of Sports and Leisure Sciences established (June)
- Ph.D. in Education inaugurated (August)
- Patsy Rooney Powers bequeaths more than $7 million, largest single gift in university history (September)
- Barry connects to INTERNET and becomes one of the nation's first universities to make it available to all users (December)

1992

- Cor Jesu Chapel refurbished; new altar blessed in honor of Thomas P. "Tip" O'Neill and his wife, Mildred
- Treasure Coast building dedicated (February)
- Damage inflicted by Hurricane Andrew estimated at $300,000 (August)
- University debt refinanced in largest transaction in Barry's history
- NCAA-II national championship captured by Barry University women's soccer team for second time in tournament's five-year history

1993

- Women's soccer team captures third NCAA-II national championship
- U.S. Attorney General Janet Reno addresses 600 graduates (May)
- Barry inaugurates BLISS, computerized library system, thanks in part to a $250,000 grant from the Knight Foundation
- SACS accreditation reaffirmed

In the fall of 1999, Barry University welcomed Sister Arlene Scott, OP, as director of Mission and Ministry, and Father Scott O'Brien, OP, as associate minister. Their roles are to provide counseling and fellowship to the students and to celebrate the sacraments. While they provide guidance to students searching for a religious life in the Catholic tradition, they also provide ministry and prayer for students who want to worship in their own tradition. Sister Arlene works with Barry's Interfaith Committee. Father O'Brien prepares members of the Barry community for the sacraments of initiation, and works to promote greater sensitivity to and enthusiasm for diversity.

1994

- Former Massachusetts Governor Michael Dukakis featured as Mideast Peace Conference draws 700 guests to Barry
- "Pockets of Pride," a campaign designed to improve neighborhoods surrounding Barry University, unveiled
- First University Homecoming weekend held (February)
- School of Human Performance and Leisure Sciences established
- Completion of the Lillian Rooney Powers and Samuel J. Powers, Jr. Human Services Building
- Completion of Natural & Health Sciences Building

Attending the meeting of the Barry University Board of Trustees on May 10, 2000 were (standing from left): Michael Griffin; William Heffernan; John Bussel, Sister M. Carleen Maly, OP; Olga Melin, Donald S. Rosenberg, Esq.; Brian E. Keeley; Albert E. Dotson; Gerald W. Moore, Esq.; Sister John Norton Barrett, OP; Vivian A. Decker; Sister Nadine Foley, OP; Frank Crippen; Tim Czerniec; Sister John Karen Frei, OP; Dr. J. Patrick Lee; and Michael O. O'Neil, Jr. Seated from left: William E. Fenton, Jr.; Sister Peggy Albert, OP; Sister Jeanne O'Laughlin, OP; Charles Modica, chairman; Leslie Pantin, Jr., co-vice chairman; R. Kirk Landon, co-vice chairman; Sister Janet Capone, OP; and Sister Candace Introcaso, CDP. The meeting took place at the offices of WXEL-TV, Channel 42 in Boynton Beach, Florida. WXEL merged with Barry Telecommunications, a subsidiary of Barry University, in August 1997.

LEFT: This photo, taken for the 1990 President's Report, celebrated the end of Sister Jeanne's first decade as president and Barry University's fiftieth year. Under her leadership in this period, Barry added two doctoral programs, developed the seventh School of Podiatric Medicine in the United States, doubled undergraduate majors offered from twenty-five to fifty, and tripled graduate programs. Student enrollment increased from 1,740 to 5,900 and SAT scores increased by 110 points. Buildings increased from sixteen to forty; the budget increased 400 percent and Barry ended each year in the black.

1995

- Barry homepage launched on the World Wide Web
- Barry ranked in top quartile of American colleges in the southern region by *U.S. News and World Report*
- Honorary doctorates bestowed on Jaime Cardinal Ortega Alamino, Archbishop of Havana, and Fr. Timothy Radcliffe, OP, Master of the Order of Preachers
- President Bill Clinton, wearing a Barry University sweatshirt, appears on the cover of first-ever *Barry Magazine*
- Ninth Barry University David Brinkley Award for Excellence in Communication awarded to Ted Koppel; ceremonies broadcast nationwide on C-SPAN
- Doctor of Ministry (Barry's fourth doctoral degree) initiated
- Sister Trinita Flood, third President (1974–1981), dies
- Students, faculty, and staff form "World's Largest Red Ribbon" for World AIDS Day fund-raiser
- NCAA-II national championship won by women's volleyball team

1996

- Volleyball player Marya Morusiewicz named NCAA Woman of the Year for the State of Florida and Top Ten finalist nationally
- Ph.D. in Nursing offered as Barry's fifth doctoral degree
- Bucky, new athletic team mascot (a Buccaneer parrot), adopted
- Inez Andreas resigns as chair of the Board of Trustees after 20 years; Charles Modica, entrepreneur and educator, becomes chair
- 1,519 new trees are planted on campus
- Hon. William Lehman attends dedication of new building named for him; located in the Lehman Building are the University Archives and Historical Collections, where his Congressional papers are housed

This august group gathered February 26, 1985 on the happy occasion of the dedication of the Andreas School of Business building. From left: former U.S. Secretary of State Henry Kissinger, who received an honorary degree that same day; Inez Andreas; the Most Reverend Edward A. McCarthy, Archbishop of Miami; and Edward Swan, member of the Barry University Board of Trustees.

1997

- WXEL-Channel 42, of Boynton Beach, merged into Barry Telecommunications, a subsidiary of the University
- Former president Sr. Dorothy Browne, OP, third president (1963–1974), dies
- Sr. Jeanne featured in four-minute "Window on America" segment of CBS *Morning News*
- Former site of the Biscayne Kennel Club purchased by Barry University and the thirty-eight acres are renamed "Andreas Park"
- Migrant Education Consortium for Higher Achievement (MECHA) funded by $3 million grant from the United States Department of Education

1998

- Religious freedom promoted by Sr. Jeanne and other religious leaders who go to Cuba after Pope John Paul II's visit there
- University debt restructured in $22 million bond issue; Standard & Poor's BBB rating received and $9 million in new revenue generated
- Barry University athletes tied for third place in the NCAA Division II race for the Sears Directors' Cup, which is considered higher education's ultimate award for overall sports achievement
- Barry University rated number one in diversity among its peers in the South by *U.S. News and World Report*
- Bachelor of Liberal Studies classes in School of Adult and Continuing Education televised by WXEL-TV
- Largest new class in Barry's history admitted; freshman and transfer enrollment increased by 77 percent over fall 1997
- Volleyball star Janina Morusiewicz '98 top-10 finalist for NCAA Female Athlete of the Year, matching feat of her sister Marya, in 1996
- Master of Science in Information Technology offered as first graduate degree in School of Adult and Continuing Education

Approximately 650 undergraduate students live on campus in residences such as the Renee Mottram-Doss Hall (shown here) which opened in June 1990. However, unlike the other seven residence halls, Mottram-Doss was designed to maximize privacy providing on-campus apartment-type accommodations for about one hundred students. Each four-bedroom suite sleeps eight and surrounds a common kitchen, dining room, and living room. Each residence hall has at least one resident advisor, a senior student trained in community development and crisis management, along with a network of peer advisors (a group of seniors living in the halls).

Barry's business students listened intently on November 30, 1999 as Edward Iacobucci, President and CEO of Citrix Systems—a Florida-based Fortune 500 company—discussed his personal experiences as an entrepreneur going into business.

1999

- Sand in My Shoes Award, the Greater Miami Chamber of Commerce's most prestigious recognition, is given to Sr. Jeanne O'Laughlin
- Purchase of newly renamed Barry University School of Law completed
- Barry University specialty license plates sold by Florida tag agencies
- Sixth Biennial Dominican Colloquium hosted by Barry University
- Florida Athena Award, which recognizes companies that make significant contributions to the professional advancement of women in the workplace, bestowed on Barry University by Greater Miami Chamber of Commerce

1999 *(continued)*

- Title III Grant valued at $1.75 million won by Barry University to create undergraduate "Center for Excellence in Teaching and Learning," to raise technological skills of faculty and students
- Sister Jeanne O'Laughlin selected by Governor Jeb Bush as one of three 1999 inductees into the Florida Women's Hall of Fame
- Dr. George Wanko, 62, senior vice president for student services, dies
- Barry University becomes first school in NCAA history to host dual championships in men's and women's soccer simultaneously; minute-by-minute results and pictures broadcast worldwide over Internet

In 1989, Barry University celebrated a noteworthy event—its first national championship. After an undefeated season, Melinda Derden Resse proudly displays the NCAA Division II Women's soccer trophy which the Lady Bucs cinched by defeating Keene State of New Hampshire in a 4–0 victory on the Buccaneers' home field. The women's soccer team went on to win the championship again in 1990 and 1993.

2000

- First commencement at Barry University School of Law
- As Barry University enters the third millennium, the work begun six decades ago by the four founders continues. The faces and voices change as faculty members and students pause here briefly, then move on to new roles and new challenges, but Barry University remains constant and dedicated to expressing those principles established so long ago—love, leadership, learning, and faith.

The Barry University women's volleyball team won the 1995 NCAA Division II National Championship. Pictured left to right: Marya Morusiewicz, named top-10 finalist NCAA Female Athlete of the Year the same year; Mickisha Hurley, who will play on the United States Volleyball team at the Olympics in Sydney, Australia in 2000; and Wei Liu, American Volleyball Coaches Association All-American in 1995.

OPPOSITE: It was a happy day for ACE student Dr. Bernard Chaikin as he and his fellow students celebrated his graduation in August 1995. The fact that he was ninety-four years old not only made it a very special accomplishment; it demonstrated that Barry University serves all segments of its community regardless of age.

INDEX

ABOUT THE AUTHOR

Prudy Taylor Board

Prudy Taylor Board is a native of Florida and a graduate of the University of Florida who has devoted much of her professional life to preserving the history of her beloved state. She is now a resident of Delray Beach, FL.

As a freelance journalist and novelist, she has had more than a thousand articles published in regional and national magazines. She was a staff writer for the *Fort Myers News Press*, assignment editor and reporter for the CBS and NBC television affiliates in Lee County, FL, managing editor of two regional magazines *Lee Living* and *Home & Condo*. She also edited *The Fiction Writer*, a magazine for writers distributed nationally. Currently she is Managing Editor of the Dartnell Corporation's sales publications and personally edits *Sell!ng* and *Sales & Marketing Executive Report*.

Her first book, *Lee County: A Pictorial History*, was published by the Donning Company/Publishers in 1985. Her novels, *The Vow* and *Blood Legacy*, were published by Leisure Books and PocketBooks. Donning published her most recent books: *Pages From The Past*; *Historic Fort Myers, FL*; *Venice, FL Through the Years*; *The Belleview Biltmore Hotel: A Century of Hospitality*; *Mending Minds, Healing Hearts*; *History of the Florida Sheriffs Youth Ranches* and *The Renaissance Vinoy: St. Petersburg's Crown Jewel*. Her next book for Donning will be the history of the Port Royal Club in Naples, FL.